Terry

by Shirlee Monty

WORD BOOKS
PUBLISHER
WACO, TEXAS

Grateful acknowledgment is made for permission to reprint the following: Page 88, the poem "Leave it all quietly to God" by Ruth Bell Graham, from *Sitting by My Laughing Fire,* copyright © 1977 by Ruth Bell Graham, used by permission of Word Books, Publisher, Waco, TX 76796. Page 107, lines from "Stopping by Woods on a Snowy Evening" from *The Poetry of Robert Frost,* edited by Edward Connery Lathem. Copyright 1923, © 1969 by Holt, Rinehart and Winston. Copyright 1951 by Robert Frost. Reprinted by permission of Holt, Rinehart and Winston, Publishers. Page 127, lines from "Those Were the Days," words and music by Gene Raskin, TRO—© Copyright 1962 and 1968 Essex Music, Inc., New York, N.Y. Used by permission.
Scripture quotations identified TLB are from *The Living Bible, Paraphrased* (Wheaton: Tyndale House Publishers, © 1971) and are used by permission. Quotations marked NIV are from The Holy Bible, New International Version, copyright © 1978 by the New York International Bible Society. Quotations identified NASB are from The New American Standard Bible (copyright 1960, 1962, 1968, 1971 by the Lockman Foundation).

ISBN 0-8499-2944-X
Library of Congress catalog card number: 81-52528
Printed in the United States of America

To my father:
Who died when I was eleven years old
But still left me a wonderful legacy—
A love of Christ,
A love of people,
And a love of writing

Contents

Foreword

> Though we travel the world over to find the beautiful,
> we must carry it with us or we find it not.
>
> *Ralph Waldo Emerson*

When I first met Terry Meeuwsen, I was struck by the fact that here was a woman who appeared to have everything in the world going for her: beauty, intelligence, loads of talent, and lots of good solid common sense.

During my travels as Miss America, I made a July 4th guest appearance in Tulsa, Oklahoma, for the Bob Hope "Stars and Stripes Show." The New Christy Minstrels were also appearing, so I shared a dressing room with the three women, all talented professional singers. I particularly noticed Terry and started talking with her, and we immediately struck up one of those quick friendships. We both came from small towns, families that were close, and we both enjoyed performing.

Terry had presence on and off stage. She'd be great material for the Miss America Pageant, I thought to myself. I knew that the people in Atlantic City who run the show steered away from the professional types, but this young woman had inner warmth, charm, and wholesomeness.

I met Terry again in Fond du Lac, Wisconsin, on one of my very first appearances after my year as Miss America. We had a chance to visit that evening and I like to think that my encouragement helped her to go on to become Miss America of 1973.

Soon after our meeting, Terry entered and won her local competition, then took the state crown, and finally became a strong contender for the Miss America Pageant. In fact, she literally wiped them out in Atlantic City.

And this is where we caught up together again, as I was co-hosting the pageant for my third year.

We ran into each other several times during her year as Miss America, catching up on our lives, our experiences, and old friends we had mutually known. Yet, it wasn't until we were both living in New York in the same apartment building that we became really close friends. It was comforting for each of us to know that we had a friend to confide in, chat with, and tell the stories of our daily experiences.

It was a time of ups and downs, of tears and triumphs. Ultimately, Terry left New York to move to Los Angeles for more studying and auditioning. I stayed in New York.

I feel this is a revealing book about the highs, lows, the successes, the sorrows, changing moods and attitudes of life and environment—the things that encompass a woman who appears to have the world by the tail, but finds new and significant things about herself and life as she grows older and wiser. Her story and experiences should be very helpful to anyone who reads the book. In short, she's a great role model, and needless to say, her tremendous faith has been her guiding light in life.

Phyllis George Brown

Introduction

She was a Miss America but is a down-to-earth genuine Christian lady. For that reason it pleases me to be able to introduce Terry's life story. It is an invaluable story of ups and downs, highs and lows, and lessons well learned . . . the hard way in most instances.

Terry tells her story with an honesty that is seldom seen. We are often anxious to share the good parts of our lives and the victories, but it is not so easy to share the defeats and the low spots when there seems to be no way to go but up. This book is written in such a way that it relates to anyone who reads it—young and old, male and female.

Terry tells how she accepted Christ as a young woman but let her commitment fade under the pressures of the world. Many of us can identify with her experiences of getting away from what is right, and how sin finally dulls our senses, causing us to forget that what we're living is wrong. Terry's life is proof that God continues to work with us even when we aren't aware of it.

When Terry shares her faith with the crowds in our City-wide Crusades and Prison Weekends all over the country, she has an astounding impact, because *she is real.* She is equally effective with the super straight and the criminals.

You will be blessed as I have been by this true life story of Terry Anne Meeuwsen.

BILL GLASS

A Note from Terry

Like most of you, I am a composite of all the people, places, and things that have touched my life. The most lasting influence has come from the people who cared . . . grandparents who prayed for me; parents who loved me through some pretty unlovable stages; and friends who have listened, laughed, cried, shared, and when necessary, forgiven me. Each of you has touched my life in a unique and special way, and I love you for it.

But the real story here is of one person's struggles and disappointments, and of a God big enough and loving enough to reach down and change her . . . not because she was special, but because He really cares that much. *"Behold! old things pass away and all things become new" (2 Cor. 5:17).*

Author's Preface

I sometimes think of Jesus Christ as a giant, roving hand that moves over countries and cultures, gently reaching down and touching lives that are dead and bringing them back to life.

He knows no boundaries. He touches young and old, rich and poor, brilliant and illiterate, men and women, all races, all colors. He touches drug addicts and congressmen, movie stars and lonely housewives, hardened criminals and wealthy businessmen, troubled teenagers and beauty queens.

One late night in March of 1971 He reached into a restaurant in Plainview, Texas, and touched a young singer on her way up. She was nearing the end of her second year with the New Christy Minstrels, a prestigious folk-singing group.

AUTHOR'S PREFACE

At twenty-two, she had already accomplished most of her professional goals. She had a successful night club career behind her. She had traveled internationally, recorded seven albums, and appeared on national television.

And yet she felt empty.

The Christian girl with whom she was eating that evening suggested that it might be because she didn't know Jesus Christ. As the young singer listened, her doubts turned to hope. And that night, she committed her life to Jesus.

What happened next? "He reached down and touched me," she said. And as she sang a year later in front of 16,000 spectators at the 1972 Miss America Pageant, "nothing, no nothing was ever quite the same."

This is her story.

Part One

TAKE MY HAND, LORD

Take my hand, Lord.
I can't make it alone.
        The hills are steep,
        The valleys deep.
I need you, Lord, to lead me on.

Take my hand, Lord.
Keep me on your path.
        I've drifted off into those woods,
        Those dark and menacing woods.
Somehow, You helped me back.

Take my hand, Lord.
I need your strength,
        Your firm hold, your gentle touch,
        Your love that gives so much.
I need You, Lord, to carry on.

Take my hand, Lord.
I keep looking back with dread:
        Full of guilt, self-doubt,
        Recrimination for my life.
Keep me looking straight ahead.

Take my hand, Lord.
Keep me in your tow.
        Don't let me stray.
        Don't let me fall.
Hang on. Don't let me go.

Shirlee Monty

Miss America 1973 (Photo © Leininger, De Pere, Wisconsin)

1.
On the Road

> Thou hast made us for thyself, O God,
> and our hearts are restless until they
> find their rest in thee.
>
> *St. Augustine*

The young singer was Terry Anne Meeuwsen. In 1972, she swept into Atlantic City as Miss Wisconsin and left a week later with a crown, a title, a $10,000 scholarship, a $7,000 wardrobe, and a chance to earn $100,000 during her reign as Miss America, 1973.

Hundreds of newspapers and magazines shouted their approval:

"She has dazzled the whole nation. She's attractive, polished, talented, friendly."

"She radiates a confidence and isn't afraid to express her beliefs."

"All grace and charm throughout the hectic pace of the Pageant."

"One of the strongest contenders since Yolande Betbeze, Miss America of 1951."

But two years before, when she was singing with the New Christy Minstrels, she was not all grace and charm.

She remembers the day she was approached by the other two girls in the group and told that she was "selfish, two-faced, hypocritical, and impossible to get close to."

"Although this sent me off on another indulgent, self-pity trip, I knew they were right. My career, my success, and my talent were my number one concern. My whole world revolved around me. *My friendships were the same way. I was interested only in what I was going to get out of them. Everything in my life was directed to making me feel good. My career was definitely headed uphill, but the rest of my life was rapidly going downhill.*

"Life with the New Christy Minstrels was not what it seemed. Those sweet, innocent, apple-pie kids were actually taking drugs, drinking a lot of alcohol, and leading a pretty heavy life-style. But when we got on stage, we put on our all-American masks, waved our flags, and did our thing.

"One of the things we did during our closing number, 'Everything Is Beautiful,' was to go into the audience and pass out pictures of the group and little buttons reading 'New Christy Minstrel Power.'

"One night following our show at Harrah's Casino in Reno, Nevada, I noticed a strange-looking guy sitting against the back wall. With his long hair, a beard, old clothes, he looked rather out of place in those plush surroundings. But I smiled, handed him a button and a picture, and was a bit startled when he handed something back. It was a pamphlet—'The Gospel of St. John'—and I said to myself, Oh, one of those Jesus freaks. Great! I give him my thing. He gives me his.

"I really thought that was the end of him but the next night he was back, with three more strange-looking kids.

This time he waited for me after the first show. When I came off stage he greeted me like a long-lost friend. 'Pssst! Terry, come here a minute. My friends and I would like to talk to you.'

"Terrific, I thought. Cornered by four Jesus freaks in the middle of Harrah's. It could only happen to me. Aloud I said, 'Hi, it's nice to see you again.' He quickly introduced himself as Phil Rothberg and said he had something to share with me.

" 'Hey, I'd like to,' I lied, 'but I've got another show in one hour and—'

" 'No problem,' Phil broke in, 'it will only take about 15 minutes.'

"I knew I was trapped, so I agreed to go next door to a club where Chico Holiday was performing. I didn't know Chico but I had heard him a couple times and I was aware that occasionally he would alter the lyrics. For example, in 'Bridge Over Troubled Waters,' instead of 'I will lay me down,' he would sing 'Jesus can be found.' I had half wondered if anyone ever complained. After all, he was hardly singing to a Sunday school crowd.

"Anyway, Phil went up to Chico, asked for his key and escorted us to Chico's dressing room for our talk, which involved something called a personal relationship with Jesus Christ. I was pretty turned off by the whole conversation. I let them know that my life was glamorous and exciting. I was on my way to the top and things were just fine. And as quickly as I could, I retreated to Harrah's and the solitude of my dressing room. But as I sat in front of my make-up mirror and studied my reflection, I didn't see glamor and excitement.

"I saw a lonely, empty shell, an aching void. I buried my face in my hands and sobbed."

2.
The Commitment

> When someone becomes a Christian he becomes a brand new person inside. He is not the same any more. A new life has begun!
>
> *2 Corinthians 5:17,* TLB

"My life was a little like a mountain stream. It was moving along swiftly and steadily, but the hills were so steep and the trees so thick that I couldn't see where I was going. I couldn't see where I would come out.

"And then suddenly, the trees were fewer, the sun began peeking through, and there in the distance, in the bright sunlight, I saw the end: my reason for being. It was Jesus Christ and I found Him in Plainview, Texas, which was our next stop.

"Almost at once, I sensed a difference in Plainview. First of all, it was our first performance at a church-affiliated college. Although we had performed all over the world and had sung for many colleges, this one was different.

"We were told that there was a rally before the show

and Linda, a new girl in our group, went over early to give a testimony. I didn't even know what a rally and a testimony were. I discovered that a rally is like those Billy Graham things on TV and a testimony is—heaven forbid!—getting up in front of hundreds of kids and talking about Jesus Christ and what He means in your life.

"Then I discovered that Rick had gone over to the rally, too, and I thought, There is no way that Rick, the swinger in our group who dates everyone from the Hertz Rent-A-Car girl to the maid who cleans our rooms, is going to get up and talk about Jesus Christ. Later I was told that he went over to put in an equal plug for our show and to make sure the rally didn't last too long, and I thought, That figures!

"Again when we hit the stage that night, we were aware of something different. There was an excitement in that audience that we'd never seen. We weren't sure if it was from the rally or if they were 'up' for the show.

"And their responses were puzzling. If we mentioned religion or God, they began clapping and shouting 'A-men.' But our really good material, the off-color stuff, got no response at all.

"When we took our final bow, we gave the peace sign, which was very 'in' at the time. Every hand in the place responded with a raised index finger. That really confused us.

"Our banjo player whispered to me, 'What does it mean?'

" 'I don't know,' I said. 'Must be a new sign. Let's give it back to them.'

"This really threw them into a shouting, stomping mood and we decided that the sign meant we were 'number one' and they really loved us. We ran off the stage to thunderous applause.

"The applause had hardly died down before kids were knocking on our dressing room doors, asking if we'd been 'born again' and were we 'saved'? Again, the confusion. 'Saved from what?' we asked.

"Before they could answer, we excused ourselves and escaped to a local drive-in, starving and ready to unwind from our performance. As we walked into the restaurant, I couldn't believe it! There they were again, the evangelist and his entire team. I headed for a back booth, hoping not to be disturbed.

"I was just glancing over the menu when a young girl slid into the booth and introduced herself as Jeannie O'Connell. Feeling really irritated, I looked up, and there was the sweetest, most peaceful face I had ever seen. 'Hope you don't mind,' she said, 'but I'd love to hear about you and your travels and everything.'

"I warmed up to her right away, of course. Talking about me had always been my favorite subject. So I told her about my exciting life, my travels, the huge crowds, the big lounges where we headlined. And yet all the time I was talking, it bothered me to know that she seemed to have it all together. She seemed to have the inner peace, not I. And I was not only three years older, but I had an exciting life, public recognition, a great future. Why should I be the one to feel empty and confused? Why shouldn't she?

"Rather unexpectedly, she turned serious. Looking me straight in the eye, she asked me, 'Terry, are you a Christian?'

"For some reason, I wasn't threatened by the question, but yet I wasn't sure what to say. 'I—I don't know,' I floundered. 'I think I believe in God.'

"She smiled. 'You see, Terry, part of the word Christian is Christ.' She went on to explain not what had to be changed in my life, not what God didn't like about me, but how

much He loved me just the way I was, with all the hang-ups, insecurities, and problems. And she told me that if I would turn all that over to Him, along with all the other areas of my life, He would change what needed to be changed.

"She talked about a personal relationship with Jesus and spoke of Him as though she knew Him. We talked about the promises He makes, the difference between the Old and New Testaments, and the second coming of Christ, things of which I knew little or nothing.

"When we parted a few hours later, she handed me a booklet called 'The Four Spiritual Laws' and asked me to have breakfast with her at 5:30 A.M. before our 7:30 flight.

"Back in my room, I tried to sort out all the things we had talked about. My pride told me it was all too simple. I needed something more intellectual, more philosophical, more sophisticated. I mean, asking Jesus to come into my heart was so easy, so personal, almost embarrassing.

"I began to leaf through the booklet Jeannie had given me. Just curiosity, I told myself. I read some of the Scripture passages. It said . . . that God loves me and that He has a wonderful plan for my life (John 3:16 and John 10:10).

. . . that because God is holy and man is sinful, there is a great chasm between the two (Rom. 6:23).

. . . that man is always trying to bridge the gap by being good enough, doing good things, but that God has already provided a way for us to reach Him, His Son, Jesus Christ. (Rom. 5:8 and 1 Cor. 15:3–6).

. . . that I must individually receive Jesus as my Savior and Lord before I could know and experience His love and plan for my life (John 1:12 and Eph. 2:8–9).

"I wasn't sure if I believed all this or not. But as I sat alone in that hotel room, I knew one thing. If what Jeannie

had told me was true, if the Bible really said all those things and if Jesus could love me in spite of what I was, I needed and wanted Him to be a part of my life.

"So I asked Him, a bit tentatively, perhaps even cynically, to come into my life . . . if He really was there.

"The next morning I had breakfast with Jeannie and I shared with her my commitment and asked dozens of new questions. As we parted I raised an index finger and asked, 'O.K. Jeannie, what does it mean?'

" 'You mean you don't know?' She looked surprised. 'It means one way to salvation through Christ.'

" 'Not that we are number one?' I laughed.

" 'Not any more,' she yelled after me. 'You've just been replaced!' "

3.

Getting in the Race

> Now glory be to God who by his mighty power at work within us is able to do far more than we would ever dare to ask or even dream of—infinitely beyond our highest prayers, desires, thoughts, or hopes.
>
> *Ephesians 3:20,* TLB

In September of 1971, the Christy's were still singing "Everything Is Beautiful," but for Terry it was more like "Where Have All the Flowers Gone?" The euphoria and the luster were getting lost in managerial problems, the rigors of road life, disillusionment with a free-swinging life-style and the anonymity of being part of a group.

"I matured a lot with the Christy's. I strengthened my voice and developed a stage presence that comes only with experience. But I reached a point where I was marking time. I was finding it impossible to make individual contacts. The Christy's were a group. That's what people came to hear and there was no opportunity for individual advancement."

Terry quit her $6,000-a-year job with nowhere to go but

a tentatively formed Gospel group and a fleeting thought about re-entering the Miss America Pageant.

As a high school senior, Terry had won the Miss Green Bay Pageant and moved on to become second runner-up to Miss Wisconsin. But a second try would involve a year of hard work, an investment of thousands of dollars, and the potential problems of perhaps being too old and too professional. It was no easy decision.

She sought advice from Virginia Habermann (now Duncan), producer and director of six Miss Wisconsin pageants and an advanced speech and modeling teacher at John Robert Powers Modeling Agency in Milwaukee.

Ginny's first introduction to Terry had been as a judge for the Green Bay Pageant in 1968. A few years later, when Terry was singing professionally at a Green Bay nightclub, Ginny and her husband arranged for a better-paying and more prestigious job for Terry in Milwaukee. It was in Milwaukee, when Terry moved in with the Habermanns, that their long friendship began.

Ginny advised against a second try, claiming that the odds were 70,000 to one, that it was a step backward and that, having sung professionally, she should continue in that direction. Terry argued that she was interested in the scholarship money that was available, as well as the experience and exposure. Further, many other attractive avenues were no longer compatible with her recent commitment to Christianity.

By November, Terry had made up her mind and on Thanksgiving Day, she called Ginny and asked for her help.

"Ginny said she'd do it but we'd have to go all the way. I thought all the way meant giving 100 percent. To Ginny, it meant 250 percent. She drove me to a degree I could never have driven myself.

"At times, I thought she was an absolute tyrant, an unrelenting slavedriver. But today, I look back and realize what a tremendous influence she was on me, and I have to acknowledge the fact that I could never have won without her.

"Probably the most remarkable thing about Ginny was her ability to involve so many people in this pursuit and not only to involve them but to build a team, a nucleus. These were people who could help me—hairdressers, clothing store owners, make-up people, pageant people. They not only helped me; they jumped on the bandwagon, encouraged me, and pushed me. It was as if my challenge was their challenge. They wanted to see if we could beat the odds, if we could do it. And along the way, we all became good friends. I really meant it when I said later, 'I didn't win this alone. We all won it.' "

Ginny acknowledges the fact that Terry got a lot of help. "Of course, she had contacts and knew people who could help her. It's true that most girls in this situation know someone, someplace, who knows what it's all about. But a lot still depends on what you do with the help. Terry was the one who had to handle the interviews, talk to the press, and walk out on that stage alone.

"And yet there was something unique about Terry. She just has that kind of personality that makes people want to do things for her. There wasn't a person who didn't go way beyond his or her contractual agreement to help her. Why, Terry had more things given to her than most states could afford to buy for their contestants."

Among the givers was Angela Quade, owner of Honey's Bridal Salon, who practically "gowned" Terry from the first pageant through her reign as Miss America.

"I lost count, but she must have given me 75 gowns,

including the $2,000 gown I wore for the Miss America competition. It was trimmed with four kinds of white lace and 9,000 beads and sequins which were hand-set by a team of six seamstresses in her store. It was absolutely exquisite.

"Her generosity was incredible. She gave me a different nightgown for every night I was in Atlantic City so I'd feel like a queen. And she gave my mother five outfits to wear at the pageant—one for every evening. She had a heart of gold."

A bonanza of daytime outfits came unexpectedly during a visit to Betty Johnson's Boutique in Thiensville, Wisconsin.

"They had elegant-looking clothing but way beyond my budget. My mother, Ginny and I were in the dressing room wondering how we could ever pay for them when the owner of the store, Bonnie White, suddenly appeared. She had called the president of the Ginori line in New York and told him that she had the next Miss America in her store and would he like to outfit her for Atlantic City?

"I'll never know why the president of a company would say 'Yes' to a woman he'd never seen in a little town he probably never heard of, but he did. He even offered to send other outfits if they didn't have my size! All he asked was for me to acknowledge where I got them, should the press ask."

Equally generous was Junior House, which contributed a Four Seasons wardrobe to the state beauty queen as well as almost unlimited access to additional outfits.

Other decisions and preparations faced Terry as she began her long journey to the Miss America Pageant. What local pageant should she enter? Green Bay again? Terry decided they might resent a second try so she opted for Appleton, instead, a small town close to Milwaukee where she hoped to work weekends. To meet pageant requirements she enrolled at the Fox Valley Technical College in Appleton since she wasn't a resident.

The next problem was how to make some money. As a part-time student and with no specific job qualifications, Terry decided against seeking steady employment.

"Consequently, I learned to live very frugally that year, meeting my expenses with part-time modeling jobs, television commercials, product narrations, unemployment compensation, and a small personal loan."

Weight was another problem.

"I had reached 160 pounds with the Christy's and I literally didn't recognize myself anymore. So I began the standard regimen: diet, fruit juice, exercise, bicycling."

She worried next about the speaking demands that would be required in her quest for the crown.

"I knew I needed some practice and I thought high school students would make good guinea pigs since they probably hadn't had any more experience than I. After leaving the Christy's, I had taken a ten-day trip to Israel so I thought it might be interesting to compare Israeli and American life. Two of my high school teachers agreed to let me talk to their English and American Problems classes. I was terrified, of course. I would try to gesture and couldn't even keep my hand still. And yet, I felt really good about myself afterwards—very pleased that I had taken the initiative and forced myself to do something that was difficult for me, that didn't come easily.

"As I look back now, I was probably a disaster, but it was a beginning. And that, to me, is the battle with anything: taking those first few steps, starting to go where you want to go. Once you've done that, the dread is over, you've conquered your fear, you're still alive, and you know you can do it.

Another imminent decision involved Terry's talent—the choice of a song.

"I felt that my talent was the best thing I had going for me so it was terribly important to pick a song that was right. I loved Barbra Streisand and thought seriously about doing 'Free Again,' a very emotional song. I liked it musically but it's somewhat sad and cynical, and I began thinking that not everyone could relate to the bitterness, the pathos of a lost love.

"I finally chose 'He Touched Me,' a much more uplifting song. I felt that more people could relate to it since almost everyone has fallen in love sometime in their life."

Terry sailed through the Miss Appleton and Miss Wisconsin pageants with hardly a ripple of competition. A close friend said, "Terry prepared for these pageants like some girls prepare for the Miss America Pageant. She knew the judges would expect more of her because she was older and was making her second swing through the contest."

Terry herself felt a bit more pressure the second time around.

"Actually, of all the interviews, the Appleton one was the hardest. It was fairly obvious that I had moved there primarily to compete in the pageant. I was older than most of the girls, I had sung professionally, and they wanted to know why I was there. When they asked why I wanted to be Miss Appleton, I didn't fool around with a lot of contrived answers. I simply said because I wanted to be Miss America. Then they asked me why I wanted to be Miss America and I was able to explain that I was interested in the scholarship program and the future opportunities that the pageant offered.

"The Wisconsin interview went much better as the first question they asked was whether I thought the swimsuit

competition was irrelevant, if it ought to be removed. Since I had just won it the night before, I said, 'If you think I'm going to tell you to get rid of it after last night, you're crazy!' That broke the ice. They all started laughing and from then on, it was just a fun conversation."

The two months following the Miss Wisconsin Pageant were filled with frenetic activity: opening shopping centers and fairs, participating in neighboring state beauty pageants, practicing poise at a model agency, taking care of last minute shopping, putting up with dozens of fittings, and finding time for talent rehearsals.

Terry described her feelings the night before she left for Atlantic City:

"It had been a long, hard year but when it was time to go, I went without looking back, without giving anything a second thought. I felt like a racehorse that had been exercised, fed and groomed for a year. I was ready to go. I didn't want to lose the feeling of exhilaration and anticipation that I had right then. I thought to myself, You've all taught me a lot and now I'm ready. I don't want to sit in the classroom anymore. It's time to get out and see what I can do."

4.

Pageant Week

> In a race, everyone runs but only one person gets first prize. So run your race to win.
>
> *1 Corinthians 9:24,* TLB

Bert Parks called it "the largest Cinderella contest in the world." Feminists refer to it as "an outdated myth, a sexist plot with meat market mentality." Terry Meeuwsen calls it "the best vehicle I could have taken to fame, connections and enough money to pay for private music and drama lessons in New York." But no matter what you call it, thousands of girls enter local pageants every year, hoping to sing, dance, or charm their way to that coveted and lucrative title of Miss America.

Terry arrived in Atlantic City on September 3, 1972 with 14 pieces of luggage, a chaperone from Racine, a mentor from Milwaukee, 150 Wisconsin supporters, a song called "He Touched Me" and a fierce determination to win.

"The atmosphere was electric: photographers, the press,

the immensity of Convention Hall, fans greeting us in our hotel, receptions, rehearsals, pictures of us everywhere, banners, posters, buttons, pageant booklets. It was unreal, like a lovely dream, and yet with monumental pressures."

Pageant week began officially on Tuesday evening with a parade along the Boardwalk before 50,000 spectators. The state queens sat on the backs of open convertibles, sandwiched among 35 high school marching bands and 25 glittering floats and presided over by Grand Marshal Joe Garagiola.

"The parade was the fun thing before all the pressure began. It was our first public appearance and by then, people had bought pageant books and knew who we were. Thousands of people were lined up, eight deep, along the Boardwalk, and they would call out 'Hi, Terry!' or run up to the car and shake my hand and wish me luck. It was very, very exciting!"

The next three days were filled with preliminary competitions: bathing suit, talent, evening gown, and that feared seven-minute interview.

"I suppose the real apprehension about the interview was whether they might throw you a curve. There is just no way of knowing what it's going to be or what they're going to ask.

"I was the first girl to be interviewed so I set the pace and in some ways, that was an advantage. And yet, because all of us contestants were a little uptight . . . after all, our interviewers weren't pageant people and some had never judged a pageant before . . . our conversations never went beyond a surface level.

"We talked about safe things like family, home, the sort of things you list on your pageant sheet. It was an easy interview and I didn't like that. It wasn't particularly

interesting or challenging. I didn't feel I had a chance to talk about what was really important to me."

Terry swept her preliminary competitions by winning both her swim suit and talent events, strengthening earlier rumors that Wisconsin might at last have a winner. Ginny was even more certain: "When Terry came out a double winner, I just knew she had it sewed up. She would win."

Terry felt she also scored high in a twenty-minute session during which the girls mingled with the nine judges, in a cocktail party atmosphere.

"Ginny advised me to pretend I was having a party and that it was up to me to introduce people, put them at ease and make sure they were having a good time. It's called externalizing, concentrating on them. We also looked up some background material on each judge so that I'd have a couple questions to ask.

"It really worked. I felt quite relaxed and I was able to break away fairly gracefully to move around and talk a few minutes with each judge."

Perhaps one of the heaviest burdens during Pageant Week is borne by the chaperone, that enigmatic figure who hovers in the background of each contestant, serving as maid, receptionist, manager and confidante. According to the Precepts of Conduct for Contestants, the girls were to be accompanied by a chaperone at all times, no parties, no smoking in public, no going to restaurants where alcohol is served, no speaking to men, including family, unless chaperone is present, no men in rooms, and so on. Happily, they were relieved of one duty the year Terry competed. Chaperones were no longer required to interrupt and interpret remarks to the press with "what she really meant to say was—"

Terry acknowledged that a chaperone can have a lot of

influence on a girl's disposition and performance during Pageant Week.

"They are with you almost all the time, except backstage at Convention Hall, where the Atlantic City hostesses take over. They are with you in your hotel, they make sure you get to and from rehearsals, help you dress, plan your schedule, take phone calls. They have a lot of delicate responsibilities: delicate, I say, because the pressures and tensions are so high.

"Some chaperones are low-key and soothing but others are prima donnas and add a lot of pressure to an already tense situation. I know many girls who didn't get along with their chaperones and had a tough time coping and staying on top of it. I was fortunate to have Barbara Best from Racine, whom I had known since the Green Bay Pageant in 1968. Barbara always treated me like an adult. After all, I wasn't eighteen. I was twenty-three and had a boyfriend who was thirty-six. She once said to me, laughing, 'Terry, how do I tell a thirty-six-year-old man that it's time to go home?' "

Terry recalls being the most uptight about the talent competition.

"I guess that was because I considered my talent my strong suit, the thing that really meant the most to me. I decided that if I couldn't be Miss America, I'd at least like to be in the top ten, which would give me a chance to sing on national television. I had always performed as part of a group or duo. And now, to be able to perform alone, to do my own thing, on that huge stage with a thirty one piece orchestra before thousands of people and millions of television viewers was just the ultimate. It's what I'd been working for all year."

Pressure is another big problem during Pageant Week.

Pressure which, according to Terry, was "beyond anything I had ever imagined: intense, unrelenting, an inseparable part of you all week."

"Actually, Ginny gave me a lot of good advice on handling pressure. She told me not to worry about or try to compete with the other girls, not to even think about winning or losing, but instead always to concentrate totally on the moment, on what I was doing and in trying to do the very best I could. She told me to take whatever energy I had and to use it positively, to send it out to the people.

"On stage, this is particularly important. You must focus on what's happening around you, not on yourself. Many girls defeat themselves with an introspective attitude. You've all seen the plastic smile, the rigid position, the mechanical movements. A tornado could come along and those girls would still be standing there. Ginny emphasized that you need to react to things when you're on stage, just as you would anywhere. If the emcee cracks a joke, you laugh. You don't just stand there, wearing the same expression."

The 1972 Pageant seemed to usher in the beginning of a new look, an awareness that it was time for change, time for the pageant to become more contemporary. One change was the elimination of the onstage question-answer period for finalists.

"We found that the questions were inevitably stupid and inane," Albert A. Marks, Jr., director of the show, remarked. "We wanted to do away with the misconception that we take ourselves too seriously. We didn't want to be a guide to all young Americans. We just wanted to present a composite."

So instead of the questions, the girls were given twenty seconds to introduce themselves at the beginning of the show.

Another major change allowed the winner to be chosen from a field of ten semi-finalists, rather than five finalists, as in the past.

"We realized that, before, by the time the first runner-up was announced, she was virtually ignored while all eyes raced to the new Miss America," Marks said.

The reigning Miss America, Laurie Lea Schaefer, made this observation concerning the 1972 Pageant: "The girls that year were more in tune with what was going on. They didn't have stars in their eyes. They were more serious. They weren't so giddy, and there was a lot less giggling. They were simply there to get a job done."

Terry probably exemplified this new image as much as any girl there. From the moment she arrived in Atlantic City, she emphasized the opportunities available through the pageant's scholarship program and its importance as a forum for young America to express its optimism and dedication, rather than simply its glamour as the superbowl of beauty contests.

Terry's own social concerns were the subject of much of the press coverage that week: the engraved POW bracelet she wore, signifying her concern and commitment to the American prisoners of war and their families; her work with VIVA, a group with direct mail route lines to North Vietnam, which pleaded for fair treatment for POWs; and her adoption and financial support of a Hong Kong child and later an eight-year-old boy from Thailand.

This social concern for those less fortunate than herself and her eloquence in speaking of helping other people made a tremendous impression on both the press and the judges and prompted one newspaper to write, "Miss Wisconsin possesses a maturity far beyond her twenty-three years."

In spite of a pageant ruling against wearing jewelry onstage, Terry was the only one of several girls wearing POW bracelets who didn't remove it.

"I considered it a commitment. When you put the bracelet on, you were committed to wear it night and day, without removal, until the serviceman was either released or some notification of his survival was given by Hanoi. I didn't consider it an ornamental kind of thing and I wouldn't have taken it off. Apparently, the pageant people agreed with me because nobody ever brought up the issue."

Even though Terry was rated an early favorite who had overwhelmed the judges in two preliminary competitions, she wouldn't allow herself to assume she was in.

"As a double winner, I was in the best position to win, but something could always happen. I just wouldn't let myself take it for granted."

Before the show Saturday night, she and Ginny talked a long time on how to approach it, how to hold on to the momentum and concentration.

"We relied on prayer a lot all week and that night we prayed together again: not to win, but to be able to handle a loss should it come and to be able to go on in a positive way and not to be crushed or devastated by it.

"After we prayed, we embraced and just looked at one another for a moment. And that final look said everything. It said that this was a year that neither of us would ever forget, that it would always be very special to each of us and that now we would be going our own way again, in new and separate directions.

"It said, 'Good Luck' and 'I'll do my best.'"

5.
Miss America

Faith sees the invisible, believes the unbelievable, and receives the impossible.

It was 8:00 P.M. Saturday night, September 9, 1972.

The television lights were on, cameras were zeroing in on the stage, Gless Osser and the Miss America Orchestra finished the overture, sixteen thousand spectators leaned forward in their seats and fifty nervous girls began their twenty-second introductions.

"Hi. I'm Debbye Hazlewood from Magnolia, Arkansas. I'm twenty years old and I'm in pre-pharmacy at Southern State College."

"Hi. I'm Constance Anne Dorn from Kinston, North Carolina. I'm eighteen years old and I major in special education at East Carolina University."

"Hi. I'm Terry Anne Meeuwsen from De Pere, Wisconsin, America's No. 1 Small City. Commitment is the most

important word in my vocabulary because I firmly believe that one man is no more than another if he does no more than another."

Terry acknowledged that her introduction didn't exactly follow the norm.

"I guess I'm always trying to be different, but I think people are more interested in knowing what I stand for, what I believe in, than in how old I am or what school I attend. So I decided to use my twenty seconds to tell them something important to me.

"I did something else a little bit differently that week. Normally, the pageant people write the talent introductions. These might come out, 'And here is Terry Anne Meeuwsen, Miss Wisconsin, singing her own rendition of 'He Touched Me,' or, 'The musical Oliver *was one of David Merrick's best productions. Here's Susie Swartz to sing 'Where Is Love?'*

"I didn't want to just fall in line with everyone else. I wanted to set the scene so that by the time I came out, they knew where I was going without my taking them there. So I asked and received permission to write my own introduction—maybe the first time it had been done, I don't know. At any rate, rather than a statement, I felt that a question to the audience might be better. It might make them sit up and listen and think about it. It had to be very short so I wrote, 'Do you remember the first time you fell in love? Well, here, expressing that feeling with a song, "He Touched Me" is Terry Anne Meeuwsen, Miss Wisconsin.' "

The introduction notwithstanding, Terry's talent performance was probably one of the highlights of the pageant. The cheering audience rose to its feet in the first standing ovation in pageant history.

The newspapers described it in glowing terms:

"Miss Wisconsin got right to the heart of the audience with her rendition of 'He Touched Me.' "

"Miss Wisconsin handled this difficult song with exceptional warmth and tenderness."

". . . excellent stage presence and a well-modulated voice."

". . . a singer with tremendous vocal range."

Bert Parks said later, "I was thrilled at her rendition of 'He Touched Me.' She really touched me, and for the first time in many years, I predicted the right Miss America."

Terry described another break during her talent presentation:

"I was number nine of the ten finalists, which meant I came on right after a commercial. Two girls would perform, followed by a sixty-second break, then two more girls, and so on. This meant that I had to stand in the spotlight for sixty seconds waiting for my introduction, and sixty seconds can be interminable at a time like that.

"I'm terribly nervous until the music starts. I worry that I'll forget the words; I get sick to my stomach; all kinds of things go on. But with the music, my fear disappears and I get lost in the song.

"It's incredible, but the soundman happened to be the same one I'd met a few years earlier when the Christy's were on the Johnny Carson show. When I saw him, I said, 'Charlie, if you'll just let me wait here until Bert gives my introduction, I promise you I'll get to the spot and be ready to go.'

"He knew I was nervous, and he held my hand and said, 'Don't worry, you're going to be great. Everything will be fine.' And he let me wait there until just a few seconds before my music began."

Terry described the tension during those final moments

before Bert announced the winner as almost unbearable.

"Photographers were lined up six and seven deep all along the runway. As Bert Parks began his announcement 'Ladies and gentlemen, we've reached the moment we've all been waiting for,' we instinctively joined hands. I could hardly breathe as the names of runners-up raced past my ears.

"And then: 'Ladies and gentlemen, one of these six ladies is our new Miss America.' I prayed, Oh Lord, grant me the serenity to accept the things I cannot change. Then I heard Bert saying, 'Our new Miss America—Terry Anne Meeuwsen, Miss Wisconsin.'

"I was stunned. All the tension and emotion of a year surfaced. I reeled under the weight of it, feeling almost drugged. Someone moved me to center stage. Suddenly I was walking down the runway, half-conscious of Bert singing 'There She Is.' Flashbulbs were going off like fireworks and thousands of people were standing and cheering and waving wildly at me. All I could think of was, Please, Lord, don't ever let me forget who I am or where I've come from."

Barely off the runway, Terry was asked what it meant to be Miss America. Her response was quoted in newspapers all over the country:

"To me, it means an opportunity, not only to further my education, but to share some of the beliefs and ideals that I formed during my travels throughout this country and around the world.

"And one of them is this: Love is like a basket of five loaves and two fishes. It never begins to multiply until you begin to give it away. And on behalf of fifty girls, I want to thank you for giving it to us this week."

Later Terry described it in more personal terms:

"Once I got past the excitement and the sheer disbelief that all this was really happening, I think that winning the

Miss America Pageant was an affirmation to me that I could reach a goal, that with enough effort and determination, I could accomplish my purposes in life.

"I found that winning was very strengthening to my spirit, very conducive to my personal growth. We all need injections of success in order to grow. It doesn't have to be a beauty pageant. It can be success in anything—in your home, an office, anywhere—just anything that makes you feel really good about yourself and inspires you to move on."

The Cinderella story has several endings.

There's the one where everyone returns to who they were at the stroke of midnight.

Then there's the television edition which ends with the newly crowned Miss America being surrounded and embraced by the forty-nine other contestants.

And finally, there's the real-life version. That one ended at about 4:00 A.M. with Terry trying to make some sense out of a handful of contracts while her chaperone-godmother stayed up all night packing her bags.

And instead of dancing all night with Prince Charming, this Miss America was alone: posing for hundreds of photographers, sitting on a daïs for hours at the Coronation Ball, roped off from family and friends, and finally, escorted by a contingent of security guards back to her hotel.

Terry laughed about all the hoopla that went on.

"I felt like I was either wearing the Hope diamond or had just been elected the President of the United States. But seriously, you can't get too carried away with it all. You have to stay a little detached. After all, midnight does come eventually, even if it's a whole year away!"

6.
Feelings

> They that wait upon the Lord shall renew their strength. They shall mount up with wings like eagles; they shall run and not be weary; they shall walk and not faint.
>
> *Isaiah 40:31,* TLB

"I guess I entered my year as Miss America with the same exuberance and expectation that one enters marriage, a new job, or motherhood. I saw all the joys and benefits but none of the pitfalls.

"With great confidence, I announced my intentions to the press: 'As Miss America, I would like to add dignity and purpose to the crown and to present the pageant in its proper light: as a scholarship foundation for talented women.'

"But by the end of my reign, I just wanted it to be over. There were joys, of course. But there were also tremendous pressures, compromises, and perhaps even feelings of being exploited. I was also very sick at the end of the year.

"I suppose the hardest thing for me to handle was the pressure of trying to be something that people expected

me to be, always playing the role of Miss America and never feeling free to just be me. It was like being on stage for a whole year and almost forgetting who I was.

"I also found myself being compared to other people, as if I were suddenly some sort of standard. I would be signing autographs and a kid would come up and say, 'I just wanted you to know that I'll never understand how you got to be Miss America. Miss Texas is much prettier than you and she should have won.' And there was the man who waited a long time in line after a banquet just to tell me, 'I must be the luckiest man in the world because you're Miss America and my wife is much prettier than you.'

"I was often up at 5:30 A.M. to catch a plane, to catch another plane, to get where I was supposed to be. I would arrive exhausted, my make-up half gone, and I would be met by hundreds of people, a band playing, and Miss Arizona, or whoever, looking absolutely gorgeous, like a Breck commercial.

"I would just be devastated, knowing that people were comparing the two of us and knowing there was no way of explaining that I'd been on the road for months with exhaustive schedules and appearances. So I'd wind up feeling more insecure and intimidated and maybe even put-upon.

"And it wasn't just the beauty thing. Very often, I would get letters after being somewhere, saying, 'You were everything we wanted you to be' and again it reinforced the pressure to measure up to someone else's estimation of what I ought to be. Almost unconsciously, I began to compromise my own individuality and to deny my real feelings to be whatever Miss America is supposed to be.

"Of course, my Christianity should have helped cushion my frustrations and maintain my perspective, but as I look back, I realize that the two biggest threats to our faith are

overscheduling and the lack of Christian fellowship: a body of believers to keep us in tow spiritually.

"I can't say my basic values ever changed. My Christianity was still very important to me. It was still number one in my heart but no longer number one in my life. I read my Bible but quality time with the Lord was practically nil.

"It was a year of selfishness, of feeling that I was the only one looking out for me. A year where my career took precedence in my life again. A year where I made compromises, subtle attitudinal changes that none would have noticed but me.

"It was a year of people saying, 'Terry, I got you X number of appearances for this month at so much per appearance and we have two separate $1,000 appearances which will really bring the money in . . . and Terry, somebody called from New York and they want you to look at some of the classical things that are being done in theater . . . and Terry, a telegram came from somebody in California who wants to make you a star. He said to contact him when the year is over.'

"And I realized that I was very interested in how much money Terry could make and what Terry would do when the year was over and what was going to happen to her career and what opportunities would be available to her. And I was too busy and preoccupied with myself to just drop down on my knees and ask, O God, what do you want me to do when this is over?

"Another problem during the year was that sometimes I felt exploited, even by the Christian community. I would often speak to youth groups and at churches and after two church services and a Sunday school class, we would go to a special restaurant with special reservations with thirty selected members of the church, so for me, it was still an

appearance. I was still Miss America. Then we would stop at a hospital to visit some of the sick members or at a parishioner's home to relax, and all afternoon, their friends and relatives would drop in. And they truly meant well; it was offered as a gift of hospitality. But when you're with people you don't know all afternoon, it's not relaxing.

"Even when I went home to be with my family, I felt like I had to be Miss America. They were understandably proud. We would visit relatives and friends, go out for dinner with these people, or have people dropping in at the house.

"So I guess that the pressures got to me and it began to feel like a year when everyone wanted a piece of the pie and there wasn't much opportunity to refuel.

"There were times when I felt so exhausted that I had nothing more to give. And there was the frustration of not being able to explain, of not being able to tell people what I was feeling without sounding ungrateful for a really exciting experience.

"If I could go back and do it over again? I'd take better care of myself. I would take off at least one weekend a month with no commitments.

"And I think I'd take more time for me: time alone in my hotel room to prop up my feet, read a book, or do my needlework. That's all."

7.

The Reign

> We need to be careful not to confuse activity with accomplishment.
>
> *Zig Ziglar*

"Dear Miss America—"

They offered their congratulations, requested autographs, asked for money and a few offered suggestions.

> Dear Miss Meeuwsen,
>
> I should congratulate—but I cannot do this.
>
> I don't think you were the most beautiful girl in the contest and I don't think your talent was the best either. I really don't know as to why you were chosen to be Miss America.
>
> I just want to be honest—because nowadays even your best friend does not say the truth.
>
> And look at your picture with the president of USA. Don't you think your dress looks horrible?
>
> And your hair? How come you did not fix your hair? Miss Schaefers dress and hair was much more elegant, to tell you the truth. Your outfit was a "granny" outfit and has nothing to do with eleganze or taste at all.

Please, try to improve the image of Miss America—don't wear dresses like that and don't look so very plain and ordinary. You are a tall girl, so why wear those platform shoes?

What does your mother say about this?

Terry's father also came under fire.

Mr. Joseph Meeuwsen:

I only wanted to tell you that you are mentally not normal in carrying for yourself and for your family such a silly, foolish, grazy name, nobody is able to pronounce right. Newspapers, TV are working hard to explain such a silly conglomerate of words.

You live in an english speaking country, why not make it easy for all of you to have a name, anybody can repeat or read.

Why not immigrating to the Congo or Tibet? People over there will welcome you with this silly, grazy name . . . What is it, any way, what does it mean?

I hope you do yourself a favor and pick a fine name anybody can understand.

The vast majority of letters, however, didn't tell Terry to get a new hairdo or emigrate to the Congo. They fully approved of the Pageant's choice of Miss America, 1973.

From her kindergarten teacher:

When you were a child, you looked up to me. Now, as Miss America, I look up to you and I'm happy at what I see; beauty, talent, love.

From a Wisconsin senator:

This will be about the fourth time in as many years that you have been the recipient of congratulations from me for some personal achievement—Miss America, of course, being the greatest! I know there will be more. You are a wonderful, talented girl.

If you should ever decide to get into politics, let me know. I'd love to be your campaign manager.

From a 7-year-old:

I watched the Miss America Pageant with my friends and we were all rooting for you.

I got a new stereo for Christmas and my mom said she would buy me your album. I think you're very pretty, talented and nice, too.

And from hundreds and hundreds of strangers:

Thank you for being beautiful inside as well as outside.

Thank you for having that special something that caught the eyes of the judges.

Thank you for that beautiful message about the fishes and loaves.

You surely did touch me—as well as millions of other Americans.

One resident described DePere the night of the Pageant: "It was like New Year's Eve. Minutes after Terry won, a stream of cars began an impromptu parade past the bungalow on East Erie Street where Terry grew up. Horns were tooting, bells ringing, lights flashing on and off."

Adding to the confusion was a steady stream of telegrams, nearly one hundred in all, including one that arrived very early in the morning. It read: "Congratulations, Miss America, from two very tired Western Union girls. Cathy and Cindy."

Terry had two of the assets that normally assured a girl of a large number of bookings: her singing and her Christian beliefs.

"Singers are always in demand because they can perform easily. There's no setting up, that sort of thing, and many functions require performances. Also, personality comes through in singing, much as it does in talking, and people relate to that.

"Christian Miss Americas make more appearances than non-Christian girls because a lot of churches have them come in as a motivational force. My mention of the five loaves and two fishes brought in a lot of requests from youth groups and Christian organizations."

Terry began her reign with a series of wardrobe fittings in New York as well as several days of publicity photo sessions for her sponsors and for the official Miss America portrait.

She also appeared on the "Today" show and faced the national press for the first time.

"It's the first time you really face the big newspaper people, the East Coast reporters, and they just fire questions at you. And they aren't easy surface questions but the real in-depth, nitty-gritty type."

From there, Terry appeared on several national television programs; Johnny Carson's "Tonight Show," the "Mike Douglas show," and "What's My Line?" as the mystery guest.

As co-chairman of President Richard Nixon's inauguration, Terry opened the program by singing the national anthem. She served in this post with Mrs. Nelson Rockefeller, because of her public support for the president.

"It was just a very, very impressive evening. Bob Hope and Frank Sinatra were the hosts, and it was overflowing with celebrities and public figures, including the Nixon and Rockefeller families."

Visiting the White House was another highlight of the year, getting to see the private quarters, an unexpected surprise.

"Every year Miss America was invited for a White House tour, but since Laurie Lea Schaefer (Miss America of 1972) and I were public supporters of Nixon, we got special treatment. They flew my mom in, so there were four of us: Laurie (who was heading Nixon's campaign in Ohio), my mother, Dorothy Schwager (my chaperone), and me. We were nervous about meeting him, expecting him to be hard to talk to and maybe a little stodgy. Finally they announced that the president was ready to see us. Going into the Oval Office was like being in a picture postcard: the carpet with the insignia, the big desk, flags on either side and the president standing behind his desk, waiting to receive us.

"Anyway, he turned out to be just great, very funny and a tremendous personality. He spent about twenty minutes with us, showing us around the Oval Office, pointing out artifacts from the heads of other countries. Then we went outside where the Press was waiting. Since Tricia had just gotten married in the Rose Garden, the president took us on a tour of the grounds and talked about the wedding.

"Next, a guide was supposed to take us on a tour of the White House, but the president said, 'Mrs. Nixon is gone, so why don't you take them through the private quarters?' and that was the best part of the whole thing. It was fun to see the way it was decorated, very yellow and sunny and bright, and to see Julie's needlepoint pillows on the couch, which had been the subject of recent magazine articles."

Probably the real "high" of any Miss America's year is her homecoming, when she is recognized and honored by those who have helped her along the way, by those who really care about her. This is the time when the crowds are full of familiar faces: friends, relatives, teachers, neighbors, pastors and priests, who share stories, revel in the glory, and glean a little credit for their hometown girl who made good.

Terry was honored at three consecutive homecomings: the first at Oshkosh, site of the state pageant; Appleton, where she won the local pageant, and De Pere, her hometown. Governor Patrick Lucey added more prestige to the occasions by designating Sunday, October 22, as "Terry Anne Meeuwsen Day" in Wisconsin.

"I think I vacillated that whole weekend between anticipation and excitement and pure, unadulterated exhaustion. The three days included a state press conference, a city-wide all-service club luncheon, a huge, elegant Miss America Ball, two parades, a full musical production culminating in the transfer of the Wisconsin crown to my successor, a reception at the library, and a dinner, followed by 'This Is Your Life' with a dozen surprise guests. I gave speeches, sang, danced, laughed, cried, waved, shook hands, exchanged small talk, struggled for names, hugged, kissed—everything but wash my hair! Incredible as it may seem, I couldn't find time in three days to wash my hair!

"There were times I felt drained, almost in a state of collapse, and in one situation, I guess I really did succumb to the pressure. It was during the Miss America Ball and they had redone the entire airport for the evening. It was magnificent. I was escorted down the stairs by a full military honor guard on a red carpet. A band was playing, flashbulbs were flashing, and there were wall-to-wall people. At least a thousand were there, including some pageant people from Atlantic City. Anyway, I stood with my dad greeting people and all of a sudden, I got claustrophobic and I turned to him, struggling to control my voice, and I said, 'Dad, I have to go now. I just have to leave for awhile.'

"My dad was talking with someone and when he said, 'Sure, honey, we'll go in a little while,' I just panicked and

my voice rose an octave and I almost screamed at him in front of all those people. Tom, my boyfriend, took me by the arm and stopped the people who were asking for autographs and weaved me through the crowd and through a side door into a corridor and I almost collapsed. I was just emotionally drained, unable to give another five minutes of myself.

"And I remember feeling very lonely out there because everyone was so caught up in the excitement and the fun of it and my parents were so proud of my position and the neat things I was doing. I had the awful feeling that nobody would ever understand the intense pressures and confusion that I so often felt.

"And yet, in spite of the pressures, there were plenty of fun times: crazy, off-the-wall kinds of things.

"I think my favorite was the time I was working in Chicago for the Gillette Company. We were often picked up by limousines but on this particular day, Irene (my chaperone) and I were picked up by the longest limousine I had ever seen, driven by two Gillette executives. It was white and seemed half a block long, with curtains all around the back section where we sat.

"When we got in, they told us to pick a restaurant, any restaurant in Chicago, where we'd like to have lunch. By this time, we had eaten in so many big, fancy, elegant restaurants that a hamburger really sounded good. So I said in a very serious voice, 'We'd like to go to McDonald's, please.'

"Of course, their reaction was total disbelief, but after a few reassurances, they drove to McDonald's, and Irene and I ordered Big Macs and French fries.

"The two executives got out of the car, lined up in McDonald's and brought us our orders. When we had finished, we opened the curtains, handed the bags out the

window, and our driver put them in the trash can. It was like doing a movie. People were staring, cars stopping, all wondering what on earth was going on. And on every trip to the Gillette Company that year, someone invited me to have lunch at McDonald's!"

There are some things that every Miss America is expected to do, and these are largely parades and pageants. Another big part of the year are the autograph sessions for the national sponsors.

"I would appear at a drug store, grocery store, or wherever they sold the sponsor's products and sign autographs for four hours. These sessions, where you were one on one with the public, were among the most demanding and draining jobs of the year. I also did a lot of print, magazine, and promotional work for the sponsors: a booklet of hair styles for Gillette, a promotional Miss America doll offer on the back of Kellogg's cereal, this type of thing."

The year ended with the seventh annual Miss America U.S.O. tour, second only to the Bob Hope Christmas tour in popularity with U.S. troops.

"I guess there were a lot of highs and lows during the tour. Highs were when we were out on the deck of a ship, another ship alongside, water all around us, singing and dancing in our little sequined, pink chiffon outfits, watching thousands of guys just having a great, great time. And the lows were those handshake tours through the hospitals where we'd see kids our own age having gone through so much, feeling the awful weight of it and always struggling to find the right words, if indeed, there were any.

"It was during the U.S.O. tour that I got so sick. By the time we reached Hawaii, I had had pneumonia and mono and I had to drop out of the show and spend a week in the hospital. It was the lowest time of my year."

But the following week, the week before she relinquished

her crown to the new Miss America, may have been even worse.

"I had releases from three doctors in Hawaii who had given me a clean bill of health and had told me I could sing and dance as long as I got enough rest. I had been asked to do so many neat things. I was invited to sing every night of the pageant as well as a special arrangement of 'He Touched Me' and 'Maybe This Time' on the final night."

However, shortly after Terry reached her hotel room in Atlantic City, a pageant doctor arrived, examined her, and announced that she was to stay in her room until Al Marks, chief executive officer of the pageant, decided she was fit to participate.

"I was just livid! I had just spent a week in a hospital room in Hawaii and I wasn't ready to sit in my hotel room for another week, particularly when I felt fine. After a series of unpleasant exchanges via our emissaries, Al called a press conference, showed X-rays of my lungs and announced that, at last, I was able to assume my duties for the pageant.

"And yet, in spite of the frustrations of those two weeks, I didn't leave with bitterness or regrets. I meant every word of my farewell speech when I said, 'It's been an extremely relevant experience for me. No other could take its place. But now it's time to move forward, to use the growth and direction gained from this year. I will . . . and I can because you touched me. You touched me, and nothing, nothing is the same.'"

8.

Questions and Answers

> O Lord God, we pray that we may be inspired to nobleness of life in the least of things. May we dignify all our daily life. May we set such a sacredness upon every part of our life that nothing shall be trivial, nothing unimportant, and nothing dull, in the daily round. Amen.
>
> *Henry Ward Beecher*

"It's very strange. One day you can shout your head off about your opinions and nobody listens. The next day you're an instant expert! People demand your views on everything from women's lib to politics to religion."

Question: Miss America, what are the girls really like who compete in the pageant? The press has a tendency to treat them all alike as if they were all cast out of the same mold.

"This is difficult to answer. Sometimes I blame the press for this—for asking vacant, stereotyped questions. And if you have grass-roots beliefs and happen to be a Christian, they really put you into a mold! But the truth is, of course, we're not all alike. Many of us are individualists even though some really are kind of nonthinkers.

"They aren't really stupid. They just don't seem to have

opinions on anything. They are the ones who like riding in parades, waving at people, signing autographs, the whole pedestal thing. And in all fairness, some of these girls are just frightened. They don't want to jeopardize their chances. Ask them if the pageant is relevant or what its value is and you get a stock answer, a chant. They've memorized their response. They're not really thinking about it.

"But I would still like to see better questions. I was always so surprised and thrilled when I was asked about things that were important to me, questions relevant to the times. I always felt that finally a reporter had done his homework, had read a little bit about who I was."

Question: Is there anything you would change about the pageant?

"Yes, I think that the ability to speak well and extemporaneously should be a bigger part of the pageant and should account for more points.

"For example, if I'm a gymnast or a harpist, I'll perform minimally the year that I'm Miss America. I'll never be asked to appear in a swimming suit, and almost everyone looks good in an evening gown.

"So that leaves speaking as something every Miss America must do everywhere she goes, even if it's for only five minutes at a banquet. For some reason, people expect a polished speaker, someone with a wealth of wisdom. If you can't pull that off, even if you have all those other things, it really doesn't matter much.

"I don't consider the swimsuit competition a cattle or meat show, but I would like to see it changed. I would prefer having each girl wear sports attire which would show another aspect of her, another interest, like a tennis dress, leotard, skating dress, or even a swimsuit. But the choice would be hers, and it would say something about her."

Question: If these girls are so beautiful and talented and motivated, why have so few Miss Americas gone on to do anything?

"I'm always amused by this question because it presupposes that anything meaningful is meaningful by your *standards, not by whether it's meeting* my *own needs and desires.*

"Frankly, I think that many girls go home and get married and are happy with that because the pressures are so intense, so bizarre that they've had enough for a lifetime. I think it's very understandable that a lot of them choose not to go on. Many are divorced which I think reflects the fact that they marry for normalcy, reacting against what they've been through. Then they discover later that they were looking for the wrong solutions to their needs."

Question: What bothered you most as you traveled as Miss America?

"Being introduced as the most beautiful girl in the country. I would just cringe when they said that because it's ridiculous. I don't really consider myself beautiful and the more I think about it, the more I'm glad I don't have to contend with that. It's hard enough, if you're doing something considered successful, to have honest relations with people. But if you're beautiful on top of that—I mean beautiful to the point of being intimidating—I don't think people hardly ever get to know you. They just accept the surface beauty and never dig any deeper than that."

Question: What was the highlight of the year?

"I know it sounds uninteresting to say this, but it wasn't meeting the president or Frank Sinatra or Bob Hope or Johnny Carson or all those other people. It was those little breathers along the way where you got to know somebody

and that person took the time to get to know you. Once in awhile we'd be in a place where we'd have a chance to really spend some quality time with people, and those were the special times."

Question: Would you describe some of the celebrities you've met? Bob Hope, Johnny Carson?

"Of course, I don't know any of them well but I have some surface impressions.

"The thing that Bob Hope seems to have achieved, which a lot of celebrities never do, is to be comfortable in the public eye. I don't think lack of privacy and being recognized is anything he sees as a problem to cope with. I asked him once how he handles walking down the street and having everybody recognize him, and he said, 'I don't handle it. If they want to talk, they have to keep up with me!' I think Bob is really what he presents himself to be: gracious, kind and infinitely patient.

"Johnny Carson was just delightful, a really charming man who went out of his way to make me feel comfortable. I must add that Doc Severinsen's band was terrific. I passed out my music and we went through it twice and it was perfect. It was exciting to sing with musicians of that caliber."

Question: What do you think about Bert Parks getting fired?

"I was very sad, very disappointed. Truly, I think it would have been more relevant to get rid of the crown and the scepter!

"Although I hate to think of anyone else singing 'There She Is,' I was far more upset by the way it was handled. I think there are private, gracious ways of letting someone go after they have served loyally for twenty-five years. And Bert was always such a gracious, kind man himself.

"As a matter-of-fact, during the pageant, the most frequently asked question was 'What is Bert Parks really like?' and I could never say enough nice things about him. He's a fun, fun man, very family-oriented and secure enough to let the girls be the stars."

Question: You seem so self-assured. Do you get nervous when you have to talk to important people?

"No, I don't get nervous if I'm going to talk. I'm much more nervous about singing. I guess I expect this to be perfect and I feel much less in control of singing than I do of speaking.

"There aren't many people that I'm awed by. I don't mean that I don't respect and admire them, but I'm not afraid to talk to them. I have known all kinds of people, and everyone I've known is struggling with his own set of problems.

"I've been in show business enough to know that glamour isn't the answer. I've known enough people with a lot of money, but whose lives are messed up, to know that money doesn't make you special. I've discovered that everyone I've known, great or famous or unique, has been pretty human and I don't feel intimidated by that.

"There is a time when I do feel intimidated and that's when I'm around someone who feels negative toward me. Not someone who criticizes me but someone who is out to make me feel threatened, who is perhaps threatened by me. I got this feeling occasionally from the press, particularly some of the women reporters."

Question: Miss America, what are your measurements?

"They add up to 94 and you'll have to figure the rest out for yourself!"

9.

Moving On

I am a promise; I am a possibility.
Gloria and Wm. Gaither

Can a small-town girl from De Pere, Wisconsin, find happiness in the hustle and hassle of New York City?

Terry went to New York in November of 1973, a few months after she had given up her crown. As Miss America, she had received a $10,000 scholarship which she decided to use for a year of study in drama, voice, speech, and dance.

"I'm not sure how much happiness I found in New York but I did endure and perhaps that's a feat in itself, particularly with all the cultural shocks: the huge apartment buildings, taxicabs, doormen, answering services, all the accouterments that are supposed to ease the strain of big-city living.

"Something as simple as finding a broom for my apartment turned out to be a hassle in New York City. I

walked into a store and said I needed a broom. It was like a Lily Tomlin sketch.

" 'Where do you want your broom delivered?' I was asked.

" 'I don't want it delivered. I need it now. I want to sweep my apartment.'

" 'But we don't have a broom in the store. Our brooms are kept in a warehouse in New Jersey.'

" 'Do you mean to tell me that I'm in New York City and I can't get a broom for my apartment? In my little town of De Pere, Wisconsin, it takes me five minutes to drive to the general store, pick up a broom, and go home, and now I'm in the biggest city in the country and I can't get a simple broom for my apartment!'

"Another adjustment was getting used to traveling by cab. It was as expensive to house a car in New York City as to pay rent for another person. So people spend their lives calling, reserving, or chasing down cabs.

"I was traveling in and out of the city a lot, doing former Miss America-type appearances, and it didn't take long to realize that a rainstorm or snowstorm could paralyze traffic, or at least turn a twenty-minute drive to the airport into a two- or three-hour nightmare.

"I recall one incident when I had a late afternoon flight out of Kennedy Airport for a speaking engagement. I was scheduled to address the graduating class of John Robert Powers Modeling School in Milwaukee that evening.

"About two in the afternoon I looked out my window and saw that a few snowflakes were coming down, so I called a cab at once. He couldn't promise me anything, so I called the doorman and told him that in case he learned that anyone from the building was going to the airport I'd like him to ask if I could share their cab.

"He called right back and said a girl was leaving in five

minutes. I threw everything in a suitcase and bolted down the stairs. By then a full-blown blizzard was erupting.

"The traffic was already bumper to bumper, and a short cut through side streets didn't help a bit. By the time we had finally plowed our way to Kennedy Airport, I had missed my flight. I spent the next couple hours standing in lines with my name on waiting lists, trying to catch another flight.

"When I realized that there was no way I could make it, I began to call people connected with my appearance but couldn't reach anyone. In desperation, I called the Milwaukee Police Department and asked if they would send someone to the graduation to explain that I was stranded at Kennedy Airport.

"I guess we all have our personal limits of frustration and I reached mine that night. I was simply unable to get into another cab and face three or four more hours of New York traffic. So instead I took a 10:30 P.M. flight to Milwaukee, stayed overnight, and returned the next day. I couldn't even think in terms of the cost. It just seemed so much simpler.

"My closest friend and confidante that year was Phyllis George. We had met years before when we were both appearing on a Bob Hope "Stars and Stripes Show" in Tulsa, Oklahoma, Phyllis as the reigning Miss America and I as a member of the New Christy Minstrels. In the following years, we'd run into one another at pageants. Then after I won, I would call her whenever I was in New York. So when I decided to study there after my reign, Phyllis found an apartment for me in her building and we spent much of that year together."

Phyllis describes Terry as "one of the great Miss Americas and one of my most favorite people in the world. I'll never forget those apartment days when we would talk about our careers, keep in touch with pageant officials and friends, laugh together, cry together, miss our families together. And Terry's tremendous faith and spirit always gave me a special lift on down days after I'd been beating the pavements, waiting for some kind of career break."

Terry, too, remembers those carefree days when she and Phyllis would put on jeans, pull their hair back in ponytails and walk Phyllis's dog through Central Park.

"We'd often just sit on the grass and talk about where we wanted to go with our lives. It's hard now for me to imagine Phyllis as a governor's wife, First Lady of Kentucky and all the things that go with that. And yet, she certainly has the right qualities: the effervescence and adaptability.

"When we were in New York, Phyllis would get a call from her agency in the middle of the day saying, 'We've got an audition for you. Can you be there in a half hour?'

"And Phyllis could wash her hair, set it, blow it dry, put her makeup on in the cab and arrive looking perfectly relaxed and bubbly, flying around chatting with everyone. It was incredible!"

Terry described her year in New York City as both intimidating and exciting: a period of growth as well as regrets.

"I discovered a lot of things about myself in New York: first, how really locked in I was with my own image. When my speech teacher said, 'Terry, I'm going to make you into a real vamp, a Colleen Dewhurst type,' I was mortified. I was hanging onto the Pollyanna, the girl next door, and it scared me to death to even consider letting go of that. But that was the potential that she saw in me and to her it was positive, complimentary.

"I also remember an incident in my acting class that made a lasting impression. We were taught by Darryl Hickman, child actor and brother of Duane Hickman.

"During one of our sessions, Darryl asked me to sing. Although no one in the class knew I was a singer, I still felt very self-conscious. But I stood up, took my semiclassical stance and began to sing.

"Darryl stopped me immediately, came over, and said 'O.K. I want you to start again, same song.'

"Only this time when I sang, he took my arms and started waving them up and down and bending my body. The class was just stunned. But as soon as my body was free of that stiff and stilted position, my voice changed and it came out big and free of tension.

"My greatest regret during that year was that I didn't audition for Broadway. At the time, I was locked into television as the up-and-coming medium, and I planned to go from New York to Los Angeles to audition for television. So I never gave myself a chance on Broadway, in spite of the fact that I had a 'Broadway voice' and all of my background was in theater, not films.

"I was also a little confused and chagrined at some of the things I was discovering about myself. I realized that I was like a lot of women today: wanting a career and success and yet being afraid of it, wondering if I could handle it; if indeed, it was what I really wanted. After all, I came from a little town where women grew up and got married and had babies. That was the thing I had seen and knew all about, and it was safe. But I also knew that I wanted more, that other thing, the career. And yet it frightened me because I knew it was different and I had to do it alone.

"What if I failed? I wasn't quite ready to leave the cocoon, completely to leave the safety of De Pere and my old life, and it showed up in a lot of indecisiveness that year.

"I remember getting a call soon after I arrived in New York from the same agent who handled Anita Bryant and

Vonda Van Dyke, Miss America of 1965. He said he would like to get together to discuss the possibility of managing my career.

"I met with him several times and I knew that Anita and Vonda were both making hefty incomes but I just couldn't let myself go that route. And I'm not sure why. Partly, I know it was because I really didn't like him very much. And yet, I think it was more than that. Had I even liked him, I think I was still afraid that I couldn't handle that, that I wasn't ready to sign my life over to someone, that I was a little frightened of success.

"When I continued to procrastinate and put off signing the contract, he just tore me apart, calling me wishy-washy and disparaging me for not making up my mind.

"I felt this same dichotomy when I was asked to sing on a show at the Hilton Hotel, which also featured Don Rickles, Pat Henry (who opens for Frank Sinatra), and some other performers. Attending were major corporations, looking for acts to book for their conventions, and of course offering excellent financial and professional opportunities.

"I sang three songs and got a fantastic response and afterwards everyone was very excited about it. But again, I reacted with, 'Let's not go too fast with this,' and I began vacillating and once more, I just never let anything happen.

"It was Socrates who said: 'Know thyself: know your strengths and weaknesses; your relation to the universe; your potentialities; your spiritual heritage; your aims and purposes; take stock of yourself.'

"Perhaps that's what I really got out of New York. I discovered some of my strengths and weaknesses and a few of my potentialities. And I began to focus a little more clearly on some of my aims and purposes."

10.
Searching for Stardom

Trust in the Lord with all your heart
  and lean not on your own understanding;
in all your ways acknowledge him,
  and he will make your paths straight.

Proverbs 3:5–6, NIV

Like most Miss America weddings, this one was *Big.* It took place on December 15, 1974 at the North Hills Country Club in Milwaukee. Headlines boldly announced "Former 'Miss' becomes Mrs." and "Terry Anne Meeuwsen Weds Steel Executive." Dozens of minor stories told about everything from her trousseau to her honeymoon to future career plans.

Guests arrived from all over the country, including the Reverend Harold Leestma from California, who officiated at the wedding, and four of Terry's five bridal attendants: her sister, Judie of Florida, Phyllis George of New York, Connie Dorn, former Miss North Carolina and Susan Bender, a former Christy Minstrel of California. The fifth was Ginny Habermann of Milwaukee.

Seven hundred guests witnessed the Sunday afternoon candlelight ceremony, which was held in the dining room of the country club, elaborately decorated as a wedding chapel.

"I met Tom about a year before the Miss America Pageant through a mutual friend. At the time, I was being considered for a product narration for his company, a fabricated steel business in Milwaukee. We dated intermittently throughout the next three years, usually with Tom flying wherever I was traveling or to New York that last year. When I decided to leave New York before Christmas, we made plans for a December wedding. However, we agreed that I would still go to Los Angeles for a year to get a feel of the television industry.

"So in February of 1975, about two months after our wedding, I moved to Los Angeles and lived with Susan Bender, who had also left the Christies and was employed by Metro Media, a rental agency for television films. I signed with two agencies in Los Angeles, Abrams Rubeloff, which handles commercial and spokeswoman jobs and the Bud Moss Theatrical Agency. Bud took me to different studios, introducing me to casting directors, and after a week, I read for a segment of a series called 'Get Christy Love.' I was cast for a small role with one line, although I was on camera more than that. The other two girls in the trio were Marjorie Wallace, Miss World, and Jaclyn Smith of 'Charlie's Angels.' Christy Love, a woman detective, was played by Teresa Graves.

"Things started out badly enough because my sister Judie was getting married on February 14 and I was supposed to be her maid of honor. When I asked if I could fly to Florida on Friday for the wedding, I was just crucified.

" 'Look, Terry,' I was told. 'You're either here to get in

the business or you're not. You can't be goofing around like this with little family functions. If you turn this down, they're not going to think you're serious and you may never get a shot at it.'

"And not knowing anything about the business, whether this was really an opportunity or not and being impressionable and wanting so badly to get something moving, I chose to stay.

"So Judie was married without me and I have never regretted anything so much in my life. She was my only sister, I would never have a chance to do something like that for her again and she was always there for me, for everything.

"As it turned out, it was an insignificant, one-shot role that never led to anything. The series itself was a bomb and was canceled soon after.

"After the 'Get Christy Love' episode, nothing much else happened. Of course, I was still doing a lot of former Miss America–type things—traveling, emceeing pageants, speaking, singing. But none of my auditions led to anything.

"I was pretty much aware of the problems at the time but there didn't seem to be much that I could do about them. For some reason, I couldn't relax at an audition. I always felt like a little girl from De Pere, slightly awed by the big city. The rejection factor was always with me. Would they like me? Did I look like I was supposed to look?

"Many of the agents were very sophisticated, very suave and I was easily intimidated by that. They would tease me about how wholesome and all-American I looked, and that always made me uneasy. I often felt I was treading in water deeper than I could handle.

"Another problem was that so many of the scripts dealt with nude scenes and four-letter words, which were both unacceptable to me. I recall walking into the office of one

casting director who, after looking at my portfolio and commenting on my wholesomeness, proceeded to gently tell me that there would be two nude scenes in this movie—one a bedroom scene and the other a rape scene. But both would be very tastefully done, he explained. I remember thinking to myself, Well, isn't that nice? It's been a long time since I've seen a tastefully done rape. And aloud I said for what seemed like the hundredth time, 'Thank you, but no thank you.'

"Another embarrassment occurred during a class in drama in which Susan and I had enrolled. Expletives were just flying around, in the scripts, in conversation, from the director. The players even inserted them in the dialogue when they weren't there, for added affect!

"Susan and I did a scene together and during our presentation, I made the same mistake twice and I said, 'Oh, shoot!'

"The director waved his arms for everything to stop and with a voice dripping with dramatic mockery, he said, 'Shoot? Shoot? Class, when was the last time we heard someone say shoot?' And of course the class broke up and Susan and I didn't go back.

"I also had trouble with something else, and again, it's a personality thing. I'm not aggressive, the type of person who stops at the agency every day, chit-chats, stops at desks, shakes hands and reminds people to keep you in mind, that you need work. I also don't go to cocktail parties and social events just to do business. And I really think that's how many people get ahead in the television industry.

"I think you have to stay after people, get to know the agencies, do the little goodwill tours, know what you want and aggressively pursue it. And I didn't do that. My attitude was, if you sign me you sign me because you think I can do something so call me when you've got work. I was waiting

for the world to come to me. And I don't think that's the way the game is played in television land.

"By the end of the year, I was feeling very discouraged and torn between wanting to go home and yet being afraid of letting go of the dream, and wondering what I was ever going to do if I did go home.

"My mother called one night when I was feeling particularly low and I said, 'I just have to find someone who knows what I believe in and accepts that,' and my mother said, 'Surely, Terry, you know someone in the business who's a Christian,' and I said, 'No.'

" 'Then what do people like Pat Boone and Dale Evans do?' she asked. And I vaguely recalled that a long time ago, someone had mentioned a guy named Art Rush who handles Dale Evans's career.

"But I had hesitated to call him. I was fearful that I might end up doing Saturday matinees, and I didn't want that.

" 'Call him,' my mother said. 'What can you lose?'

"So I called Art Rush. And I just rattled off all my frustrations non-stop. 'Mr. Rush, you don't know me but my name is Terry Meeuwsen and I'm out here looking for work and I'm a Christian and nobody understands what I believe and it's been very difficult to get work and I understand you're a Christian and that you handle Dale Evans and I wonder if we could talk about my talking to you.'

"There was dead silence on the other end of the line, then this kind of soft chuckle and Mr. Rush said, 'Miss, I'd like to help you but I'm not a Christian.'

"And even with the protection of the phone separating us, I blushed furiously and all I could think of to say was, 'Well, do you know anyone who is?'

"Mr. Rush kindly explained that he handled Miss Evans's secular appearances while Wayne Coombs handled her

Christian appearances. 'Call Wayne and tell him I told you to call,' he added before I could gratefully hang up.

"But I didn't call Wayne Coombs. My dignity had been so shattered that I couldn't risk anything else going wrong.

"That night as I lay in bed I prayed, 'Lord, what on earth am I supposed to do? Should I stay here or go home? Could you please have the minister say something in church tomorrow morning that would be meaningful to me, that would help me make up my mind?'

"The next morning when Jack Haford began his sermon, I sat there transfixed. It was as if he had sat up all night, writing his message just for me.

"It was based on the portion of Scripture after Christ's resurrection when the disciples were fishing and Christ appeared to them on the shore. They weren't catching any fish, and He told them to drop their nets on the other side. When the nets filled up, John recognized who He was and said, 'It's the Lord.' And then Peter jumped out of the boat and swam to shore.

"When the disciples had brought the fish in, they all sat down and had a meal together. Peter was on one side of Jesus and John was on the other side. About halfway through the meal, Jesus turned to Peter and said, 'Peter, do you love me?'

"And Peter said, 'Lord, you know I do,' and Jesus said, 'Well, then, feed my lambs.' After a little more time went by, He turned to Peter again and said, 'Peter, do you really love me?' and Peter said, 'Yes, Lord, you know I love you.' 'Then take care of my sheep,' Jesus said.

"Still a third time Jesus turned to Peter and said, 'Peter, are you even my friend?' and Peter said to Him, 'Lord, you know everything. You know that I love you.' Jesus said to him, 'Then, take care of my sheep.'

"The minister said that all of Peter's life he had trained

to be a fisherman. It was all he knew how to do. Fishing was his identity, his security blanket. But Jesus was asking him to be a shepherd and telling him that if he'd let go of the fishing, He'd make him a shepherd—the best shepherd that there'd ever been. But Peter had to let go of his security blanket first.

"And I knew He was speaking to me. I left church saying to myself, Oh, Lord, what am I going to do if I go home? And just then I heard a voice say 'Terry?' I looked up and there was a girl I hadn't seen for a couple years.

"She had been a friend of Linda's when I had first become a Christian and was still with the Christy's.

"When she asked how everything was going, I told her my dilemma and the things I was struggling with. 'You know,' she said, 'what you need to do is come and talk with the guy I'm going to work for next week.' 'Who's that?' I asked, and she said, 'Wayne Coombs.' And I said to myself, O.K., God, I hear you.

"So I called Wayne the next day. I made an appointment to see him and eventually signed with his agency. I returned to Milwaukee and worked with Wayne's agency for a year, speaking and singing at churches, crusades, and meetings of Christian organizations all over the country.

"Like Peter, I gave up my security blanket—my self-perceived identity—and began to let the Lord do the leading. I wasn't at all sure what kind of shepherd I'd make, but I did know one thing: if anyone could teach me how, He could."

Above: Terry as an East De Pere High School cheerleader during her sophomore and junior years (far left, front row). Left: Terry (on right) as a Theta Phi Alpha pledge on the campus of St. Norbert College (West De Pere, Wisconsin).

Above: The New Christy Minstrels. Terry, 21 years old, is in middle row, next to bass player Dan Glenn. Others (left to right) are (top row) Mike Umphrey, John Hylton; (middle row) Jere Palmer, Linda Hart, Bill Zorn; (front) Rick Hanson. Left: Terry with an old Wisconsin friend, Michael Cauldie, during New Christy Minstrels' performance in Reno, Nevada.

Terry's rainy day arrival in Atlantic City to compete in Miss America Pageant, September 1972.

"You mean I have to compete with ALL THESE GALS???????"

"Meeting Bert Parks was a special part of the week. He is a very kind and gracious man."

Terry walking the runway during the opening of the 1972 Miss America Pageant.

Left: Modeling for Ginori. Above: "Cutting up" with Phyllis George. She and Terry hosted 1977 Miss America Pageant. Below: An appearance for Gillette in Tempe, AZ, during Terry's reign. Dorothy Schwager, one of Terry's traveling companions, is on the right.

Terry's USO Troupe ran into comedian Marty Allen in San Francisco on their way to Korea and Okinawa. (Terry is second from end, top row, on left.)

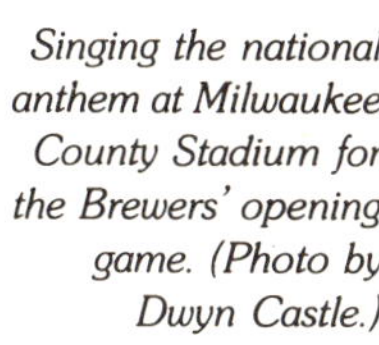

Singing the national anthem at Milwaukee County Stadium for the Brewers' opening game. (Photo by Dwyn Castle.)

Visiting with Jimmy Bakker on the "PTL Club."

Staff of Terry's WTMJ-TV show, "A New Day." Left to right, first row: Jill Bishop, director; Debbie Heid, floor director; Terry, host/producer; Budd Reth, executive producer. Second row: Tony Lucas, remote cameraman; Janet Livingston, assistant producer; Tom Ringe, assistant producer.

At work on "A New Day." (Photo © by Greg Puza.)

Part Two

DECEPTIVE DREAMS

Life's never what it's said to be—
A world of peace and laughter,
A place where happiness prevails,
Contentment ever after.

Reality is covered up
With dreams and wistful prayer.
And when the truth is finally seen,
The dream's no longer there.

Reality's in no way real,
Or so to me it seems.
Yet, how can I determine then
If dreams are really dreams?

Terry Meeuwsen, age 15

Miss Green Bay 1967, age 18, performing in talent competition at Miss Wisconsin Pageant, where she became second runner-up.

11.
Beginnings

> Train a child in the way he should go,
> and when he is old he will not turn
> from it.
>
> *Proverbs 22:6,* NIV

Several years ago, returning from a southern vacation, we drove through Plains, Georgia, and we knew at once that we were in Carter country. As I drove into De Pere, Wisconsin, a few years later, I knew almost as quickly that this was, indeed, Meeuwsen country.

From the large "Home of Miss America" sign in front of City Hall to the official Miss America portraits in public buildings to the Miss America postcards, this city of 13,000 still lets it be known that it, too, has a hometown celebrity, Terry Anne Meeuwsen, Miss America of 1973.

Four generations of Meeuwsens have grown up in this beautiful Fox River valley where the river falls over the last dam into Lake Michigan and where farming and paper manufacturing abound.

And it was here, in her grandparents' apartment building overlooking the Fox River, that Terry spent the first five years of her life.

"My parents both worked those first few years to save money for a down payment on a home, so I spent a great deal of time with my grandmother. I can remember those years as being very, very secure and the apartment house as just a wonderland for a little girl. There were elevators in which to go up and down, long halls in which to play marbles, and a basement full of furnaces, niches and cubbyholes in which to play hide-and-seek.

"Underneath the elevator was a huge storage bin with cold springs where my grandparents kept the potatoes and vegetables. My grandfather would lift up the lid and crawl in with a flashlight, and I would always be so frightened that he wouldn't come back. I would just stand there and hold my breath, looking into that big, black hole until he came out again.

"And there were wonderful things outside, too: the locks that the tugboats went through and the bridge that would go up and down and all kinds of little hiding places under the bridge.

"And I'll always remember those large cozy rooms and the grand piano and the wonderful smells from Grandmother's kitchen. But most of all, there was a warmth and love in that home that I just can't describe.

"It was the kind of home where you sing Christmas carols, where the pastor and his family come for Sunday dinner, where you celebrate birthdays, holidays, and special days with large family gatherings and where you sit on laps and listen to endless stories.

"I remember my grandfather's rich baritone voice leading

us when we sang our family grace: 'Be present at our table, Lord. Be here and everywhere adored. These mercies bless, and grant that we may feast in Paradise with Thee.'

"The table almost vibrated at that booming voice. I remember that he always switched to the harmony on the A-men.

"Whenever I think of my grandmother, I think of Proverbs 31: 'The family of a godly woman shall rise up and call her blessed.' My grandmother was blessed, indeed. As a child, I felt complete acceptance from her. In a thousand ways, she said 'I love you' every day, whether it was taking the time to play my favorite song on the piano or reading Bible stories to me or making up songs about my being her only brown-eyed grandchild. She always made me feel a little bit special.

"Discipline in those years was kind of a group effort but it was always firm and irrevocable.

"My best friend, Bridget, and I were not immune to trouble. And we both got walloped and sent to our rooms more times than I care to remember. I suppose one of our worst transgressions was the day that a lot of my grandmother's tenants had hung clothes out on the back lines to dry and it started to rain. Bridget and I decided to throw mud and sand all over those wet clothes and it was quite a mess before we were discovered and sent to our rooms, after being thoroughly blistered.

"Another time I raised my mother's wrath was when I picked a mound of vegetables out of our neighbor's garden. Although we were fenced in, I had reached through the fence and plucked every vegetable that my stubby little fingers could reach.

"My mother marched me, screaming and crying, to our

neighbor's door, where I was made to apologize. But instead of being angry, the lady felt so sorry for me that she gave me a quarter!

"Then my mother started in on her, saying, 'How can I teach her right from wrong when you give her a quarter for pulling up your vegetables?'

"When the time came for us to leave the apartment and move to a new neighborhood, I was sad and a little frightened. Some kids carry around a security blanket but my security blanket was my grandmother's house. It was very hard for me to leave it."

12.

Life at the Meeuwsens

By wisdom a house is built,
  And by understanding it is established;
And by knowledge the rooms are filled
  With all precious and pleasant riches.

Proverbs 24:3–4, NASB

"My mom? She's very warm, very unassuming. The kind of person that everyone likes. My dad is like that, too. A terrific personality, the life of the party. Wherever I go, people always ask how my parents are."

Terry's parents met at East De Pere High School. Bev Anderson was a pretty blue-eyed cheerleader and Joseph Meeuwsen a star basketball player. They were married seven years later.

Eventually the Meeuwsen household included four children: Terry, Judie, and, four years later, two boys, Joe Jr. and Peter.

Both Meeuwsens took their parental roles very seriously. "Discipline was strict but I hope not unreasonable," Terry's mother recalled. Terry and Judie had a midnight curfew on weekends, and one night when they were late, they complained that they didn't have enough time to go out for pizza after the game. Following a heated argument, Joe and I said we would check it out. After the next game, we went to the Pizza Garden and discovered they were right. They couldn't get home by our curfew so we extended it to 1:00 A.M.

"However, there were situations where we did not relent. If they were invited to a party, I always called to make sure the parents would be home. On one occasion, I discovered the girl having the party was home alone, and we would not permit Judie and Terry to attend. They were so angry, they cried and said their friends could all go and I remember saying, 'I don't care what your friends do. We set the rules and that's the way it has to be.'

"We heard the next day that so many kids turned out that they ripped fixtures out of the bathrooms, broke things, and left a terrible mess."

But most of all, life at the Meeuwsens was fun.

"My mother always went out of her way for us. She made our costumes when we were in productions; she did our hair and helped us with our make-up. She was the Girl Scout leader; she taught us all to dance; everything.

"Before we were allowed to go to public dances, she would let us have them in our backyard. We would string lights all over the place, play music all night, pop popcorn, and make Kool-Aid. Our house was the gathering place for everybody.

"And she was the kind of mom that my friends could talk to, who took the time to listen. She was very receptive and accepting of everything we said. So the kids always leveled with her. They might have even told her things they couldn't tell their own parents."

Pam Jonas, a close friend of Terry's, described the Meeuwsen home as a mini-John Robert Powers School. "Bev was so interested in the way we walked, the way we talked, what we wore, how our make-up looked, how we came across, how polite and kind we were. She always encouraged us to be the best we could. And I know that she really increased my self-confidence."

Bev Meeuwsen admitted to a lot of involvement with her children.

"Yes, I did have the girls walking around with books on their heads, teaching them to use make-up, all the things that contribute to poise and self-assurance. My mother was a beautician and she always did that with me.

"She thought it was important to learn carriage and good grooming and to have confidence in yourself. So it was always a fun thing when I had my own girls."

Sister Paula, Terry's eighth grade teacher, and Jeanne Guerin, her high school music teacher, both credit Bev Meeuwsen as giving her children excellent home training.

"There's just no getting away from it," Sister Paula said. "Even though she wasn't Catholic, she was very active at school, helping with bake sales—all those things. She is an unusually charming person."

Jeanne Guerin feels that much of Terry's self-discipline and strength came from her mother.

"Bev is a very determined woman and a hard worker. And Terry has never been afraid of work. Bev is also extremely competent and well-organized, the kind of person who is always doing things. And of course, Terry is like that, too."

Bev Meeuwsen's children are all grown now. Looking back on her years as a parent, she talked about some important things she had learned.

"When you're a parent, you can't just be a parent during the good times. You also have to be a parent during the bad times, the tough times. You have to love all the time, not just when you feel like it. And I think that's why our family survived and remains so close. We do love each other all the time and we're not afraid to express it or show it.

"And I've learned another lesson as I've struggled with worries and problems over the years. You don't have to worry. If you have a problem, you can put it in God's hands and leave it there. He can handle it and if He wants to do something with it, He will. You can trust Him with it.

"We've had our tragedies. The most traumatic was when our son, Joe, who was eighteen at the time, was involved in a felony. It was soon after Terry had won the Miss America Pageant so the story received a great deal of publicity.

"But when Joe came home, we let him know we loved him dearly, that we supported him and would stick by him through his problems. Today he's happily married to a wonderful girl. And perhaps we're all stronger because of it.

"We've prayed through a lot of things in our family. Judie was in a boating accident the summer after high school graduation. To be called and told that your daughter is paralyzed has to be the most frightening and numbing experience in the world. She stayed home for six months and gradually most of the paralysis left. She's in Florida now, happily married and the mother of a beautiful little girl. So time does heal and prayers are answered.

"When Terry was with the Christy's, she would call and tell me of the drug problems and some of their unpleasant experiences. I would just weep for her and worry and pray. And there were times I felt a distance between us, a strain, and I had to hold back my feelings and just wait for her to come back. And she did come back, with a whole new strength and purpose.

"I think we've had a very rich life and a love that has been deep and strong enough to keep us together. Our family has always been the most important thing to Joe and me. And now that we're older, we're discovering how neat it is to know they like being with us and want to include us in so many things.

"These are the rewards, the joys of having a family: discovering how much they give back and contribute to our own happiness."

13.

Whose Church?

> "Leave it all quietly to God my soul":/
> the past mistakes/that left/their scars./
> All bitterness/beyond control,/
> that mars/His peace,/demands its toll./
> Confessed to Him/ . . . and left . . . /
> it would/like all things/work together/
> for my good,/and bring release./
> I would be whole./So/"Leave it all
> quietly to God/my soul."
>
> *Ruth Bell Graham*

Have you ever wondered why we end up where we do spiritually? Why some of us become committed as children, some as college students, some in middle age, yet others live a lifetime without ever finding Christ? Why some search and struggle for answers; why some hit rock bottom before reaching out to Him; and why some are born, live and die in the same church without a ripple of discontent?

Why are some so satisfied with an almost perfunctory faith while others dig their whole lives for depth and relevancy and meaning? And why do some, like Terry, grow up with years of strong religious training, then drop out of church altogether, live for years without Christ, and then gravitate back to Him with a whole new freshness and devotion?

Whose Church?

"I don't know why I left the church or why, years later, I committed my life in a whole new way. But I do recall feelings and resentments and incidents in those early years that might help unlock the door that led to where I am today.

"De Pere is a very heavily Catholic community and I did feel some confusion about my parents going to separate churches. My dad was Catholic and my mother, Lutheran. In spite of the love and security of my home life, I was still aware of a separation—that Mom couldn't go to our church and receive the sacraments and we couldn't go with her.

"There might have been other mixed marriages in my class but I wasn't aware of them.

"I also remember thinking that although the church always seemed like a very holy environment, none of it really came together for me. The priest seemed miles away, behind a railing with his back to me, almost untouchable. And he spoke in Latin, a language I didn't understand.

"And I remember feeling almost guilty because I felt so attached to the pastor in my mother's church. My father often had to travel out of town when we were young and Mother would take us to Mass first, then to her church since Dad couldn't be home with us.

"I would sit there so excited, waiting for the end of the service because I knew the pastor would come down the center aisle and wait at the back door. And I knew that when we went through the line, he would say, 'And how are my two little angels today?' and he'd toss Judie and me up in the air and hug and kiss us and say how glad he was to see us.

"Although I was ashamed of it, I truthfully found more meaning in my mother's church than in my own.

"But an incident in the first grade probably planted a seed of resentment that festered within me throughout those first eight grades of school. It was years later before I was able to begin to resolve those feelings and begin to forgive some of the injustices that I felt.

"Only a few days after school started, my first-grade nun called me to her desk while the other children were doing their homework. 'Terry, your mother's not Catholic, is she?' she asked.

"I said, 'No, she's not.' The question didn't mean anything to me because it had never been a source of friction in our home. Mom had never tried to influence us to enjoy her church more than ours, nor had she ever dwelt on any differences between the churches.

"Sister went on, 'Do you know, Terry, that if you don't convert your mother before she dies, her soul will go to Hell for all eternity?'

"I just looked at her. I didn't know what to say. Nobody had ever said anything like that to me before. I just stood there, not knowing what to do.

"She asked me to stand on one of the reading benches and she told all the children about my mother and made them kneel down and pray for my mother's soul.

"And then she said, 'All right, I'm going to dismiss all of you for recess, but Terry, I want you to go in the corner and kneel down and pray for your mother, that God will spare her.' And I went to the corner, faced the wall and prayed for my mother.

"After I had gone home, hysterical, sobbing and shaking, the matter was resolved. The nun apologized to my mother and promises were made that it would never happen again.

"But the damage had been done. I felt, whether real or imagined, a certain alienation, a certain aloofness from the

priest and many of the nuns. When the priest came in to teach catechism, he rarely called on me, and I told myself it was because I was different.

"When a girl in my class was called to the front of the room and given a special award because her mother was a convert, I slid down in my chair and tried not to notice the smugness all over her face.

"When a nun in fourth grade discovered a compact in my pencil box and told the class I was the vainest little girl she'd ever seen, I felt the blood rushing to the top of my head until my ears pounded.

"I had never thought about it as something to make me pretty. I never thought about looking in the mirror that was inside. It was just something my mother had given me because I thought it was beautiful.

"I remember a young priest coming to our church, Father Mike, and I thought he was the niftiest priest I'd ever seen. He used to come out at recess and laugh and joke with the kids, but for some reason, it was impossible for me to joke around with him like the other kids. And I wanted so much for him to like me, yet I never felt he did.

"It was probably one of those irreversible situations where you strive for attention and you don't get it; then you try harder and get louder and you still don't get it. Meanwhile your self-image slowly begins to crumble along the way.

"So my insecurities grew and I turned into a kind of loudmouth, the one who always has to be at the head of the pack. I still recall a time when we were all riding bicycles and I just had to be out in front, making all the decisions: now we're going this way, now we're going that way. I needed that approval from my friends, that false sense of security.

"It took a lot of soul-searching and a lot of growth before I was able to resolve my resentments.

"My resentment, at first, was directed to the individuals. But as I grew older, I reasoned that it was really the church that was at fault. After all, it was at the root of these circumstances for having taught the nuns to think that way.

"Still later, as I grew in maturity and love, I exonerated both the nuns and the church and finally relinquished my case.

"As I look back today, I can see there were certainly nuns who emanated the love of Christ, who encountered our individuality, and who loved us unconditionally. And I always thanked God for those. They were the ones who encouraged my singing, gave me special art projects, and whose feelings toward me went deeper than my homework.

"My eighth grade nun, Sister Paula Baumgarten, was like that. If I had a Nancy Drew book tucked behind my geography book, she was firm but she didn't chastise me. If I didn't have my homework done, she gave me an opportunity to make it up.

"I remember feeling something for her at the time, as much as one can feel as a kid. But in the years since, I've really grown to love her, and we still keep in touch.

"I realize that today, both the schools and the church have changed. Discussion, self-expression, methods of discipline that don't destroy self-worth, openness and acceptance of other religions have all become a part of Catholic thinking. And I know, too, that a love of Christ does not allow bitterness or resentments. But this is where I came from and in some strange way, it helped make me what I am today."

14.
In the High School Pressure Cooker

> Remember, O Lord, thy tender mercies and thy lovingkindness; for they have been ever of old. Remember not the sins of my youth, nor my transgressions: according to thy mercy remember thou me for thy goodness' sake, O Lord.
>
> *Psalm 25:6–7,* KJV

Jeanne Guerin, Terry's high school music teacher, leafed through her senior yearbook, rather amused.

"There are twenty-two pictures of Terry in here! And the list of her activities is endless. Secretary of this, treasurer of that, member of Language Club, Homecoming Queen, on and on.

"I think that Terry had an unusual maturity and sense of responsibility at this age. Every teacher felt they could give her a job and it would be done, and done well. While so many high school girls were out bumming around and sleeping all morning, Terry was doing things. Even at that age, she had very definite ideas about where she was going. She was always confident, a little more sophisticated, a little more intent than her peers. Yet she was always friendly to everyone, and of course, had her own little coterie of friends.

"It was a thrill for me to have Terry Meeuwsen in the chorus because anything we did was colored by her voice. She would determine the quality of the whole soprano section. If you have one really outstanding soprano, everybody wants to imitate her and they all produce the same kind of quality.

"Another advantage of girls like Terry is that they attract boys to chorus. When Terry arrived, I had been beating the bushes to get some boys involved and most of them couldn't be bothered. They had grown up with the notion that only girls sing.

"I'll never forget the day I was walking down the hall and this big, handsome, six-foot basketball star came up to me and said, 'Mrs. Guerin, that *Sound of Music* was the neatest thing I've ever seen and the way Terry sang was about the greatest thing in the world.' Suddenly, chorus wasn't quite as boring to the guys as it had been before. So it's always nice to be able to set out your bear traps with some nice, sharp girls."

During her high school years, Terry worked as a waitress at the Village Gate. Her employers, Mike and Peggy Jelenic, remember her as a hard-working, dependable employee.

"We should have more Terry Meeuwsens around," Mike said. "She was a super waitress and a delightful girl. She was also an infectiously happy person, the kind that made everyone else feel 'up.' We always had a feeling that Terry would go somewhere, but we never dreamed she'd go as far as she has. But she had that commitment, that drive that puts certain people out in front.

"Terry and her friends worked here when the Green Bay Packers were on top, and since the players stayed in dormitories at St. Norbert College, they used to come here a lot to eat. Some of the girls would get nervous around them but Terry never had any trouble handling their humor. She could just throw it right back at them. Yet she was never a turn-off for people. She always did it in good taste."

Terry's friends acknowledge that she had drive and self-discipline, but that she was not above having a good time, or even getting into trouble.

"There was the time we threw about a dozen eggs all over the car parked next door to the Meeuwsens," laughed Pam Jonas, a close friend who lived across the street. "We must have been angry and upset about something. Boys, I suspect. Anyway, a police car was there in no time and it turned out that the car we had hit belonged to the neighbor's son who had some important papers inside which were covered with eggs! We had to clean his car, inside and out, and then, to add to our indignity, our mothers made us wash his car every week for the rest of the summer.

"We must have been fourteen or fifteen when we tried smoking. We chose Cathy Collin's garage because it wasn't attached to the house and there was a small room above it.

"About fifteen of us went up there and smoked and smoked until we could hardly breathe. I can't remember that anyone ever tried it again, at least until they were quite a lot older, but at the time, it seemed like a great thing to do."

Then there was the time that Terry, her sister Judie, and four friends stayed overnight in the high school.

"When we left the building on Friday, we put a pencil in the side door so it wouldn't lock or set off the alarm," Judie said. "After the football game, Terry's boyfriend drove us, with our sleeping bags, guitars, and food, to the tunnel across the highway from school. We sneaked through and then, one at a time, waited until there was no traffic. When it looked safe, we darted across the lawn and through the unlocked door, which fortunately hadn't been discovered.

"Safely inside, we located an upper bathroom with no windows so the lights wouldn't show from the outside. We stayed up all night singing, eating, cleaning our lockers, running around trying to get all the stools flushing at once, anything we could think of.

"Nothing was said for about three months and then two of the girls mentioned it to someone. A few days later we were called, one by one, to face not only the principal and superintendent, but worst of all, our mother, who was the school secretary.

In spite of her popularity and achievements, high school was no easier for Terry Meeuwsen than it is for most teenagers.

"I had terrible fears during those years, terrible insecurities; a lot of confusion, depression, and emptiness; a lot of sitting alone at night, looking out the window, crying. Times when nothing made sense, when life seemed to have no meaning.

"And in spite of what people saw, I was insensitive to a lot of people. I remember a girl in my school who had a speech impediment, who was naturally very shy. The guys would imitate her a lot and I would do the same thing, right to her face, and then we'd all laugh. If I could find this girl and apologize to her today, I would do it.

"Even now, I'm embarrassed at how easily and outwardly I could laugh at some of the kids or make fun of them. I think I felt that if I could get other kids to laugh at what I was doing, then no one could laugh at me. In other words, I thought I had to establish myself at someone else's expense.

"I belonged to a very 'in' clique in high school and I always felt a tremendous pressure to be accepted in this group. I

guess it's a dichotomy that we'll never quite understand: how someone can be so popular—which I was—and yet feel such low self-esteem—which I did. It's like Marilyn Monroe and Freddie Printze. They had it all. Why couldn't they be happy?

"I know, of course, that much of the reason I accomplished all those things was to earn the right to be liked. I was trying to measure up, to be important enough, to earn respect, and yet it never seemed enough. The desolation and hopelessness were still there.

"I remember an incident when I was a senior in high school that absolutely devastated me. I had been a cheerleader in my sophomore and junior years and tried out again in my senior year. I was sitting in my seventh-hour bookkeeping class when they announced over the loudspeaker who had made the cheerleading squad, and I hadn't made it.

"Later I found out that my shorthand teacher had gone to the physical education teacher and convinced her that since I was taking private voice lessons and was so involved in music, the cheering and screaming wouldn't be good for my voice.

"I had already discussed it with my mother. 'I don't care about that,' I told her. 'I'm fine. I've done it for two years and I only have one to go. I can still sing and it means that much to me.'

"But when it happened, I was heartbroken. I couldn't even go to games for a long time without having to leave at some point to go to the girls' room where I would lock myself in one of those little cubicles and just sob. And again, nobody ever knew that.

"I often wonder how we get in touch with our real feelings. How do we ever learn to share them with our parents, our

friends, our teachers, with other human beings? What are we afraid of?

"And isn't this at the heart of our problems today? The depression, the drug scene?

"And people say, in all seriousness, 'But he's from such a good family, she was such a good kid, he was an athlete, or she was a straight A student,' and all of these things are supposed to mean they're healthy.

"Parents cry out in disbelief, 'We had no idea he was on drugs' or 'Why would she ever O.D.?' And those very cries of anguish show that we are miles away, maybe even light years away, from communicating the depths of where we really are."

15.

Losing Can Be Winning

Pain is a teacher from whom we can learn much.

John Powell

In her senior year in high school, Terry was sitting in the office of a Green Bay dentist, when his nurse slipped an entry blank into her hand and began to tell her about the revived Green Bay Pageant.

It was 1967 and Green Bay had not had a pageant since 1952. The nurse, Carmen Bolger, had recently moved to Green Bay with her husband from Wausau, Wisconsin, where both had been active in the Wausau pageant. After joining the Green Bay Junior Chamber of Commerce, the two had gotten enough support to reinstate the Green Bay Pageant. Carmen must have been convincing because Terry signed up and found it was "just good fun, nothing cutthroat, no pressures. There were twelve of us and we had Pepsi parties, practiced our walking, and worked on our hair and make-up together.

"And when it was over, I had won. I hadn't seriously expected to but I was aware of really wanting it, of a sincere desire and determination to win.

"Once I had won the local pageant, everybody began zeroing in on me about the state competition. What was I going to wear? What should my talent be? How should I wear my hair?

"And the rumors began circulating about who the strong contenders were, who had the great voices, who were the best talents. Miss Milwaukee was touted as the probable winner, and there were tremendous resentments toward her before Pageant Week had even started."

Peg Jelenic, Terry's chaperone to the state pageant, saw a real change in Terry after she won the Green Bay title.

"She came back with a genuine desire to entertain, to be somebody. I think it was in Green Bay that the twig was bent. She really worked hard after that. She jogged every day, lost weight, worked hard on her talent, had a whole routine."

Ginny Habermann, director of the state pageant, agreed.

"As Miss Green Bay, Terry was a little high school girl who put on her prom dress. But by the state pageant, she had really gotten her act together. I hadn't even expected her to place, and the fact that she was second runner-up was simply amazing!"

When Peggy and Terry left for Oshkosh and Pageant Week, Peggy had never heard Terry sing.

"I had missed the Green Bay Pageant because it was held in the evening, the busiest time at our restaurant.

"On the first day of Pageant Week, Terry and I went down to the practice room and she began to rehearse her talent, a medley of songs from *West Side Story*. As she began to sing, I got goosebumps all over and tears in my eyes. I just couldn't believe that she could be so good and still be so young.

"Before I heard her sing, I felt we had come as a lark, that Terry couldn't possibly finish. But after hearing her, I realized she was a very legitimate contender, perhaps one of the strongest. And happily, by the end of the week, she proved me right."

Terry made many friends at the state pageant. She impressed the judges, was well-liked, and was encouraged to try again the following year. But she herself remembers having a very negative attitude and a lot of resentment that week.

"I made some great friends, but there was a terrible, destructive feeling among most of the contestants—an almost venomous concern with beating Miss Milwaukee. She was kind of a cloud hanging over us all week, the front runner that everyone expected to win.

"By the final night, I was in the top ten. Twenty minutes before the show began, eight of the girls came to my room and said it was up to me. I was the one who could knock Barb out of the running.

"I just broke down and sobbed. The pressure was already so great to perform for my family and friends, to be happy with what I was doing, that I just couldn't handle anything else.

"And I didn't knock her out. She won and I was second runner-up.

"I was absolutely shattered. I was young, frustrated, and immature, and I simply didn't know how to deal with losing. I was so disappointed that I couldn't even go back to the dormitory. Peg and I went to a park and I just sobbed for about an hour.

"I wasn't at all pleased that I was second runner-up. All

the resentments, gossip, and bitterness of the past week had taken away all the pleasure. There was no graciousness in me, no happiness for the girl who won. I said all the right things but in my heart there was nothing but animosity.

"Looking back now, I can see that losing that pageant was one of the best things that ever happened to me. You can only go to Atlantic City once, and had I gone that year, no one would have even known I came into town.

"And the following year, having fun as Miss Green Bay rather than struggling with the pressures of Miss Wisconsin, gave me a chance to throw off my resentments and begin to grow."

16.

A Double Life

> Happiness is like a butterfly. The more you chase it, the more it will elude you. But, if you turn your attention to other things, it comes and softly sits on your shoulder.
>
> *Viktor Frankl*

"I lived a double life the next year. I was Miss Green Bay, public relations person for the pageant, and also a freshman at St. Norbert College, a private, denominational school in De Pere with an enrollment of about 1,700 students.

"I was very secure and confident in my role as Miss Green Bay but I was insecure and intimidated as a college freshman. I could walk alone into a convention of five hundred people as Miss Green Bay and be perfectly at ease. But there was no way I could walk alone into the cafeteria at St. Norbert College.

"As Miss Green Bay, I spoke at countless conventions, was interviewed on TV, sang the 'Star-Spangled Banner' at sporting events, addressed fifty thousand persons at

Packer games, visited hospitals, and presented flowers to President Nixon when he campaigned in Green Bay.

"But I copped out on the simplest responsibilities at school.

"I had pledged a sorority and I simply avoided or ran away from anything that was embarrassing or difficult, which was what the pledge period was all about. I wouldn't go to the cafeteria because the pledges had to address the actives before they left and ask, 'Are you finished eating?' or 'Can I get you anything?' and I simply couldn't do that.

"After what seemed an eternity, the twelve-week pledge period was over. But there was so much I hadn't done that the sorority wouldn't activate me. They told me I could try again the following year, a shattering indignity.

"Another case of copping out involved a college play in which I had won the lead. However, it was a pretty heavy play and I had the role of a prostitute, a part with which I just couldn't get comfortable. But rather than going to the director and being honest about my feelings, I told him that the pageant people said I couldn't do it, which wasn't completely true. Needless to say, I didn't get another part that year, robbing myself of some valuable opportunities and experience.

"I guess as Miss Green Bay I knew who I was supposed to be and what was expected of me. But as a college freshman, I didn't have a place, I didn't know where I belonged, and I reacted with a strange combination of shyness and outrageous behavior.

"A denominational school doesn't guarantee that its students are all righteous, church-loving kids, and the ones I ran around with were a pretty wild bunch. We were all testing our new-found independence, and none of us had much idea of where we were going. We were searching, groping, restless, and all pretty much focused on ourselves.

"I quit going to church that year and wasn't even sure what I believed any more. The more I focused on myself, the more lost I became and the less direction I had. I kept thinking that if I could just sing professionally, if I could just make it in show business, I'd find all the answers.

"My life as Miss Green Bay was much more satisfying. It was there that I found the self-esteem that seemed so elusive at school. It was there that I was important, that I was somebody.

"Since the pageant I'd won was the first in Green Bay since 1952, my job was to sell the program and what it offered, as well as to orient the whole community to the fact that someone was now available to come to their functions. And I was kept busy since it was important to establish the pageant again after so many years.

"When I look back, I see myself as having been a bit of a chameleon that year. I was so young, vulnerable, and eager to please that I would take on any responsibility, fit into any role that was expected of me. I think if they had asked me to stand on a box in the middle of a supermarket and sing, I would have done it.

"I was very adept at watching other queens and programming myself as to how to act, how to handle myself, what was acceptable and what was unacceptable, the right things to say.

"I was often called upon at a meeting of perhaps a hundred and fifty people to say a few words or sing a song, without accompaniment, and I would jump up and do it, never even considering that I wasn't prepared or that I might sing off-key. I just took on whatever request was made of me and assumed that everybody did that.

"It turned out to be a year of not having any limitations on what I could do. It didn't even occur to me to be afraid

or to wonder if I was supposed to be able to do something. I didn't even think about it. I just did it.

"I'm amused now as I look back and realize how many things have come in handy in my current job on TV, things I don't think twice about because I learned to do them when I was too young to worry, too naïve to say no.

"I suppose the most traumatic time of the whole year was having to give up my crown. I had formed such strong bonds with people. It had gotten nice and comfortable and I liked being the center of attention and all the things that go with that. Phyllis George once told me that this was the way I would feel after my year as Miss America. But she was wrong. After that year I wanted to say, 'Look, any one of you fifty girls who wants this crown, just come and get it!'

"But that's not how I felt after my year as Miss Green Bay. If given a choice, I would have elected to stay. I was still too immature to want to give it up, to want to grow and move forward—mostly because I didn't know where to go. I knew that I didn't belong in college. I didn't want to teach. I wanted to perform and I couldn't learn that in a classroom.

"I had to sing professionally, but I just didn't know how to get there."

17.
The Big Break

> In every heart there is a God-shaped vacuum
> which cannot be satisfied by created things,
> but only by God the Creator revealed to us
> through Jesus Christ.
>
> *Blaise Pascal*

Once upon a time there was a tavern
Where we used to raise a glass or two.
Remember how we laughed away the hours,
And dreamed of all the great things we would do?©

"I jumped on the nightclub carousel when I was only nineteen, with stars in my eyes. I got off four years later when I finally saw how tarnished it all was—when I discovered that underneath the plastic smiles of the riders of those bright-colored horses with the gold rings were a lot of unhappy people, drinking, laughing and dreaming away the hours trying to escape the emptiness of their own lives.

"My ticket to the entertainment world was through a Green Bay pianist, Dennis Busse, whom I met the summer after college. I was working at a De Pere restaurant, The Village Gate, and Dennis had been hired to play for a private party downstairs.

"After closing, I was invited to join the party, and Dennis

and I began singing duets and having a great time. He invited me to visit The Cove, the club where he was working and offered to vouch for my age. I was only nineteen and it was a club for people over twenty-one.

"Often when I had a date, we would wind up at The Cove and Dennis would always invite me to sing. Later he asked me to join him two nights a week, then three, and it wasn't long before I was working five nights a week.

"My sheltered, small-town life showed up in an incident that took place soon after I began singing with Denny. It was New Year's Eve and when we were ready to close, one of the regulars, who seemed like a really nice guy, asked me to come to his apartment for scrambled eggs. I accepted, fully expecting to have breakfast with him. When I discovered what he really had in mind, I was furious. 'Wait a minute,' I said. 'I came here for breakfast. What kind of a jerk are you and what do you think you're doing?'

"When I told Dennis about it the next day, he was hysterical.

"From then on, the chameleon came out in me again. I began to learn how to cover up my naïveté and not let people know that I didn't understand half of what they were talking about. I learned to laugh at the right time and to pick up on clichés and double-entendres without knowing exactly what they meant. I even learned to use them myself, as well as the lingo of the barroom that showed I'd been around, too.

"Here I was, nineteen years old, hanging around with people who were forty or fifty, who had drinking problems, whose marriages were falling apart, and who came back to the club night after night—and I thought they were big shots. We'd go out for breakfast afterwards to these little

hole-in-the-wall places where steak and eggs were $1.75 and to me, this was Hollywood, this was the Big Time.

"Gradually I began to go downhill, to sink into a life that had no meaning; a life of tawdry jokes, empty laughter, and endless parties. I began to smoke packs of cigarettes, drink a never-ending supply of double scotch and sodas, and gulp diet pills as my weight shot up to a hundred and sixty pounds.

"My eyes began to look like slits as my face puffed up under the onslaught of too much alcohol. I remember nights when I drank so much that I was physically ill the next day, nights when as many as fourteen drinks would be lined up in front of me. I wasn't an alcoholic in the sense that I had to have it. But I was an indiscriminate drinker in the sense that if the alcohol was there, I drank it.

"And in spite of the bizarre life styles, the perversity all around me, I still found it glamorous, fast-moving, exciting, and exactly what I'd been waiting for. I was singing and nothing else mattered."

"Not only was Terry singing, but singing well," says Ginny Habermann-Duncan, producer-director of the Miss Wisconsin Pageant.

Whenever the Habermanns were in Green Bay, they dropped by to hear Terry and Dennis. It was Larry Habermann who found them a booking in Milwaukee with more prestige and better pay.

"We bounced around Milwaukee for almost three months, playing some really nice clubs, Fazio's on Fifth, the King's Four, the Pfister Hotel. And of course, we started making a lot of money.

"I remember one night when Dennis and I were playing the West Allis Inn and a very nice gentleman came up and requested 'My Elusive Dreams.' When we had finished, he

went up to Dennis, thanked him and tucked a bill in his hand. Dennis put it in his pocket and took it out later in the car. All of a sudden he yelled, 'Terry, that guy gave us a hundred dollar bill!' and then he just screamed, 'No, it's two hundred dollar bills!' I grabbed one and said, 'O.K. You look at one and I'll look at the other one!' I had never seen a hundred dollar bill in my life.

"Whenever this gentleman came in after that, he always requested the same song and always handed each of us a hundred dollar bill.

"Our reputation grew, and we were soon accepting bookings around the state, and even as far out of state as Des Moines, Iowa. Our longest booking was at George's Steak House in Appleton, where we drew terrific crowds and stayed on for six months.

"But in spite of our success, the growing crowds, and the abundance of money, I was happy only those few hours when I was singing.

"I continued running, grabbing at straws of temporary gratification, and using diet pills to deal with my problems. I wanted so much a life that was special, that was not run-of-the-mill. What was a meaningful life anyway? Was there really such a thing?

"And the parties went on. I was mingling with homosexuals, lesbians, drug users, people with strange sexual hang-ups, marriages going nowhere, people whose existence I hadn't even been aware of when I'd been in my little cocoon in De Pere.

"I suppose I really bottomed out emotionally at a party one night at a Green Bay motel. We were all sitting around drinking when one of the guys folded a belt in half, pretending to strike a fellow called Roy. I went in the kitchen because I didn't like the sharp, cracking sound.

"Pretty soon Roy came out, blurry-eyed, and I realized that the fellow had really been hitting him. He had welts all over his shoulders.

"I reached over and touched them. They were hot and raw. I said, 'Roy, look what he's done to you. Doesn't it hurt?'

"I will never forget the eerie feeling I had as Roy looked at me, smiled, and said, 'No, Terry, it feels good.'

"As I began to use more and more diet pills to stay high and as I found myself thinking about taking my own life and as I began to get more and more bored and sickened at the misery and perversity around me, I knew that I couldn't live like this any longer. I had to find a way out.

"And then one beautiful day when I was trying to deal with all of this, my cousin called from Chicago. She said the New Christy Minstrels were holding open auditions and if I was interested, I would need to come that night.

"I called Denny and told him I couldn't work, then headed for Chicago. I returned to work for two weeks after the audition, sure that I hadn't made it.

"Then another call came. Could I leave for Los Angeles within twenty-four hours?

"With my head spinning and tears rolling down my cheeks, I packed my bags, boarded a plane, and headed West this time—for California and a spot with the New Christy Minstrels."

18.

The New Christy Minstrels

To all who mourn in Israel he will give:
Beauty for ashes;
Joy instead of mourning;
Praise instead of heaviness.
For God has planted them like strong
and graceful oaks for his own glory.

Isaiah 61:3, TLB

In the late sixties and early seventies, America's youth were making headlines: Kent State, Woodstock, San Francisco's flower children. Dr. Timothy Leary had introduced a new drug, LSD, into a growing drug culture. The Jesus-freak movement had just started, with kids being baptized in the Pacific Ocean and pictures of Christ on the covers of *Time* and *Newsweek*. Billy Graham had written a book called *The Jesus Generation*. Folk music was beginning to fade and bluegrass rock was coming in. But groups like the Kingston Trio and the New Christy Minstrels were still pretty big on the national music scene.

"I'll never forget the excitement of being in L.A., knowing that I had made the auditions and that I was going to be part of a national group.

"Five of us were new to the Christy's—three girls and two guys—and when we knew we'd made it, we rented a little Volkswagen and drove all over Hollywood and Los Angeles, waving at everybody we saw and calling out, 'Hi, we're the New Christy Minstrels!'

"At the beginning, it was fun to be part of the group. We were all so fresh, like young colts put to pasture, and it was such a big stepping-stone for each of us. But working fifty weeks out of the year, living out of a suitcase, and trying to adjust to seven different individuals from seven different backgrounds was not always easy. Sometimes I felt like I was married to seven people I didn't want to marry.

"With three girls, there was always a clique—two friendly and one on the outside. An ugly emotional explosion took place at the end of a two-week concert in Ontario, Canada. The three of us always stayed in one motel room to save money and at this particular time, Susan was the outsider. Jere and I teased her unmercifully, calling her 'goody-goody two-shoes.'

"Susan had the annoying habit of always leaving her suitcase in the middle of the room, lying open, and we'd have to walk around or over it. One evening, when Jere asked her to pick it up, Susan said, 'Later.' We both knew that meant 'Never.'

"I was furious, so I picked up Susan's suitcase, folded it, opened the door, and threw it out on the lawn. Then Jere grabbed Susan's lamp, pulled the socket right out of the wall and threw it out on the lawn.

"By then, any semblance of sanity had disappeared and a genuine free-for-all had erupted. Everything in the room was flying out the door. There was hair-pulling, screaming at the top of our lungs, a drag-em-down, knock-em-out fight and language that would turn the most indecorous truck

driver pale. Finally, our anger spent, we calmed down enough to bring everything back in.

"The next morning, Susan and I went to the lobby to get a paper so we could read the review from our show the night before. A man, who was at the desk checking out, was saying to the clerk, 'Do you know, I was next to those New Christy girls last night, and I have never heard language like that before in my life. I sure don't know what was going on in there, but everything in the room was sailing out the door.'

"We were too embarrassed to even buy a paper. We ducked out of the lobby and went back to our room, wondering how many other people had seen our motel performance the night before. I don't think it was ever quite that bad again.

"As members of the Christy's, we did have many exciting experiences and opportunities. During one of our appearances at the Rainbow Grill in New York, David Frost was in the audience. He was dating Diahann Carroll at the time, and the two of them came backstage and asked if we would like to appear on his television show.

"They had been impressed with Jere, the black girl in our group who sang 'Oh, Happy Day,' and they asked her to sing that and the rest of us to do a group number.

"Later we did two Bob Hope 'Stars and Stripes' shows, one in Washington D.C., and the other in Oklahoma, and those were always fun as we met lots of people. I saw Bill Glass for the first time when he gave the opening prayer for the show in Oklahoma, hardly dreaming that one day I'd be appearing and witnessing in his crusades.

"Besides performing in almost every state, we traveled to Japan, Korea, Canada, and Mexico. Our first trip to Japan and Korea was a three-week U.S.O. tour and we sang mostly

in hospitals. Later, on a commercial tour of Japan, we sang in concerts, on television, and, strangely enough, in the windows of department stores. It was a bizarre feeling to have people standing around, staring at us, kind of coming and going.

"We also recorded seven albums in four languages, French, Italian, Japanese and German. A big disappointment came, however, when the owners decided to release an album in this country. Naturally, we were all excited, but then the message came that 'We're going to have studio musicians do it and when it comes out, we'll send you a copy!'

This was our introduction to a pattern that happened over and over. With each new release, we'd get a copy which would read, 'The New Christy Minstrels' even though we'd never been in the recording studio.

"It was debilitating to get into a nationally known group and not be allowed to record. Obviously, it was far less expensive for them to hire studio musicians than to detain us from our road tour.

"Occasionally, we would be embarrassed when our audiences would request something we had supposedly recorded and we didn't know the song. Then one of the owners would rush out and call a quick rehearsal to teach us the song!

"Another case in which we felt exploited was in making a film commercial for a metropolitan New York bank. The eight of us conceived the idea, wrote the jingle, and spent four cold winter sunrises in Central Park filming the commercial. It was sent to the owners of the Christy's, but we never heard another word until several months later, when we discovered they had sold it for $30,000. When we pointed out that we had done all the work, we were each given a $150 bonus!

"As naïve, impressionable young people who wanted desperately to make it, we were a little like puppets whose owners are pulling the strings. If they told us to jump one foot, we usually jumped three.

"I suppose the ultimate in programming took place in Hawaii where we had asked to be part of a large rock concert scheduled for the crater, Diamond Head.

Our request was turned down because we didn't sing rock or play electric instruments so the Christy's two owners decided to cash in on the publicity by having us stage a protest.

"We were supposed to sit outside the tunnels leading into the crater and sing for twelve hours non-stop from 6:00 A.M. to 6:00 P.M. while handing out pamphlets explaining our kind of music, the principles we stood for and the differences between the drug-free and the drugged society. We were to sing only two songs, alternating 'This Land Is Your Land' with 'Everything Is Beautiful.' The owners were to have a nurse and an ambulance on call as well as food and drink for us.

"Well, after three nightclub shows, we got up at 5:00 A.M. and trucked out to Diamond Head with all our sound equipment, but the nurse, ambulance, food and drink never arrived. One of the owners came out to watch us. While we were singing 'Everything Is Beautiful' at the top of our voices and passing out stacks and stacks of pamphlets, he sat in his air-conditioned car and smoked a pipe. We were such a big hit as far as he was concerned that he scheduled us for a repeat performance in Philadelphia. When we got there, we discovered that we were staying in a hotel which happened to be having an award ceremony that night for rock groups. Since we weren't included in the awards, he

decided we should stage another protest in the lobby of the hotel. With our protest underway, he left town.

"Our instructions were to stand in the lobby for twelve hours, singing our songs and of course, passing out our inexhaustible supply of literature. Unfortunately, this time the owners had neglected to clear our protest with the hotel management, and pretty soon they (the management), the organizers of the award ceremony, and our road manager were all carrying on heated discussions in the lobby while we were still singing 'Everything Is Beautiful.'

"People were struggling to get past us to find a seat and looking at us strangely as we stood there with our guitars, banjos, and tambourines. They certainly did not seem vitally interested in what we were protesting.

"Finally, we were told (we were still singing!) that our road manager would try to get the permit but that we were to get in the elevator and go to our rooms. But he added that we must keep singing for the twelve hours because we had advertised that fact and couldn't back down now.

"As our elevator stopped at each floor on the way up and people saw eight young people singing 'Everything Is Beautiful,' they'd take one look and go the other way.

"We finally got to our hotel room, closed the door, still singing like fools with no one even around any more. Suddenly one of the group stopped singing. 'What are we doing?' he asked. We all stopped then and just looked at each other incredulously.

"We all became rather resentful of the Christy's owners, feeling we were being used to their advantage, but I was the most shaken by a conversation I initiated one evening between shows in Reno, Nevada.

"One of the owners was sitting alone at a table and since

I was going through some struggles about myself and what I ought to do with my life, I gathered together all my courage and went over to him.

" 'This business is really important to me,' I said. 'I know you've been in it a long time. I respect your opinion, so I was wondering if there was any advice you could give me as a young performer?'

"He sat back, puffed on his pipe a few times, looking like Solomon himself gathering together all his wisdom. Then he looked directly at me through squinted eyes and said, 'Yes, I do have some sound advice for you, Terry. If I were you, I'd go home, get married, and have babies.'

"I remember looking at him and feeling like I had just put my heart on a cutting stone and he had sliced it into a million pieces. And he was going on about what a nice little girl I was but that he didn't think this business was cut out for me. But his voice was miles away and I wasn't hearing him any more.

"When I reached the dressing room, I was in tears. The other kids were furious at him. They told me that if I let one man influence me, I really should get out of the business. What did he know anyway?

"So in the end, they gave me what I had wanted to hear from him—encouragement, reinforcement, belief in myself. But it was devastating and humiliating not to have received any of that from him: on the contrary, he had dashed every bit of hope that I had."

19.

Night of Terror

> God is our refuge and strength,
> an ever present help in trouble.
>
> *Psalm 46:1,* NIV

"If I grew up a lot during those first two nightclub years, I learned a lot more with the Christy's. Perhaps the biggest difference was that this time I was with kids my own age. Drugs were in, and in spite of our wholesome, clean-cut image, we partied with alcohol, marijuana, hash, and sometimes things we'd never heard of before.

"One of these was Acapulco Gold. We went to see the Kingston Trio one night and Rick and Bill in our group knew one of their guys so we partied in their hotel room after the show. They had brought the stuff in Mexico, and we all smoked it. I don't remember another thing that happened that evening. I had only a couple puffs, but I was gone. That night simply disappeared from my life.

"We partied so much and slept so little that diet pills had become a staple in my regimen. I knew exactly how to use them to keep myself going and to stay 'up' for the long hours and endless parties.

"Drugs weren't the only thing that permeated my mind at that time. I was developing a philosophy that was against all the values I had grown up with. It was totally alien to anything my parents had taught me. I found out where to get birth control pills and entered into a series of liaisons in order to prove to myself that I, too, could be sophisticated and worldly. One of the older girls in the group felt that to get tied down or involved with a guy emotionally was a terrible threat to your career and that a relationship should simply provide physical pleasure. And to be really smart, you chose a married man, because then both of you could walk away from the relationship with no regrets. This way, she reasoned, you got all the frosting and none of the cake.

"With only a slight twinge of reluctance, I was able to embrace that philosophy, which allowed me to seek pleasure but to avoid relationships, feelings, and attachments, and callously pursue that big star in the horizon. My problem was that underneath all the bravado, I did form attachments, and I suffered through some painful, poignant moments when I had to say good-by.

"The guys in our group had even less respect for sex. Instead of a single relationship, they often had orgies. And the supply of available groupies was inexhaustible. Although none of us girls were ever actively involved in that kind of life style, technically we lived with it and assimilated it into our thinking. After all, these guys were all like brothers to us, and we laughed and joked with them and the coarseness, the emptiness, the lack of respect for life ultimately rubbed

off on us. We truly didn't see it as wrong. It was simply the way it was.

"It's strange: two things that probably had the most lasting impact on my life happened during those two short years with the Christy's, one traumatic and one joyful.

"The traumatic event was when I was raped in Hawaii, and the joyful one when I became a Christian. I hope that someday I can blot out the painful memories and nightmares of that terrible night when I screamed for two hours and nobody heard.

"We had been doing three late shows a night at a plush hotel in Hawaii following the Don Ho show. It was a two-week booking during the Christmas and New Year holiday.

"On New Year's Eve I was going to my dressing room about 12:30 A.M. to get ready for the 1:00 A.M. show. The only way to get there was through the club. By this time, everyone was very drunk. As I passed through, a Samoan fellow grabbed me and tried to kiss me.

"I knew he worked for the club but I hadn't met him and he frightened me. I pushed him aside very brusquely and proceeded to my dressing room.

"A few nights later, following our last show, the management feted us with a champagne party. Several of us, including the black girl in our group and Ben, the liquor manager who was a good-looking Samoan, got into a lengthy discussion concerning racial prejudice.

"Ben described the prejudice he had experienced when he tried to date white girls as a college student in the states. Apparently the white guys had given him a bad time of it, even to the point of physical harassment.

"I acknowledged that being from a small town, I had little

experience with discrimination. The only blacks I had known were Green Bay Packers and they were heroes. I told him it had never occurred to me that the Samoan people were also victims of discrimination.

"At the end of the evening, Ben asked if he could show me a few of the sights before the Christy's left Hawaii. The following day we were free to pack and get ready for our Japanese tour, so I agreed to go out the next evening.

"I had so much to do the next day that I thought about breaking the date, but after our discussion about discrimination, I was sure Ben would take it personally. I decided to go ahead and just beg off early.

"It was a fun evening. We went to a lot of little Polynesian bars and I was very much aware that he would march me right up in front to watch the floor shows so everyone could see us come in. We never sat in the middle or back, always right up in front.

"At another point in the evening, he almost took my breath away when he suddenly called me a derogatory name. 'Why on earth did you call me that?' I asked. 'Why did you push me away when I tried to kiss you on New Year's Eve?' he asked in return.

"And then I knew why he had looked familiar to me at the champagne party. I hadn't even remembered where I had seen him before.

" 'I pushed you away because you grabbed me and scared me,' I explained. 'I didn't know anyone there. I just wanted to get to my dressing room. It didn't have anything to do with you personally.'

"Then the subject was dropped and we resumed a friendly, normal conversation.

"Since we both worked for the same nightclub, we were staying in the same hotel, which was attached to the club.

My room was on the third floor and Ben's was on the eleventh.

"He had asked me to come up for a nightcap but I declined and pressed the button for the third floor. When the elevator door opened, he put his hand over the door and kidded me about not letting me get away without a nightcap. I repeated that I wasn't completely packed and that we were leaving early in the morning, but in the meantime the door closed and the elevator kept going.

"It wasn't a scary thing. He was charming and attractive and rather than creating a scene, I agreed to have one drink with him. 'After that,' I repeated, 'I've got to get back to my room and pack.'

"I sat on a sofa in his living room while he went to the kitchen to mix the drinks. I don't even remember him bringing the drinks or coming back, but all of a sudden, he was on top of me.

"I just froze, terrified. There are simply no words to describe the panic I felt at that moment. I've repressed much of it. I can't remember the details, but I know that I screamed and cried for most of two hours and nobody came.

"I remember trying to form words, trying to ask, 'Why are you doing this to me?' but nothing would come out. I couldn't get words together—only sounds, and they didn't mean anything.

"I had read in articles about rape that if a woman really wants to get away she can, and yet here I was and I simply couldn't move. I was totally pinned down, flattened out, and he was ripping off my dress. There wasn't a thing I could do. He bit me, choked me, and threatened to kill me if I didn't shut up. I had the eerie feeling that he enjoyed seeing me so frightened. He called me names and slapped me, and the more upset I got, the more hostile he became.

"I had always thought a rape was completed quickly and then there was sorrow and remorse afterwards. But this was slow and deliberate as if he relished every moment and didn't want it to end. It was two hours of pure panic: panic rushing up into my throat, a funny taste in my mouth from saliva glands going out of control and total inability to catch my breath enough to cry and scream any more.

"And then my whole body began trembling and convulsing and the strangest thing happened. All of a sudden, everything in me let go and it was as if I was floating. I was very, very calm, and although he was still on top of me, I thought, If I close my eyes and lie very, very still, maybe he'll think he's hurt me and he'll leave me alone.

"There was no more panic in me. There was nothing to struggle against any more. At this point, all he could do was kill me and I was ready to accept that.

"At the very end—I can remember it like it happened yesterday—he looked at me and said, 'Oh my God, what have I done to you?' and he fell off of me and onto the floor in a heap and began sobbing.

"In a series on rape that we did on my television show, a psychologist pointed out that the rape victim is in shock. Following the act, her thinking is illogical and her motor responses inappropriate.

"This helped explain my own strange behavior. While he was still sobbing, I got off the sofa and walked into the kitchen and wet a washcloth. Then I put him in bed, pulled up the covers, and washed the tears off his face. He was still crying.

"Then I found my dress and put it on, but I don't recall walking out the door or getting on the elevator. My next recollection was standing in front of a mirror in my room and seeing my face slowly coming into focus.

"Jere and Susan awoke and were annoyed that I'd come in so late. It was 3:30 or 4:00 A.M.

"I didn't know what to say. I couldn't get the word 'rape' out of my mouth so I said, 'You know, the strangest thing just happened to me' and Susan turned on the light and said, 'Oh my God, what happened to you?'

"Our television series also pointed out that after the initial shock, there is either anger or apathy. Anger is more positive. It involves letting out the emotions while apathy results in withdrawal, giving up, blaming society for not protecting you.

"My reaction was apathy. I had the feeling that it didn't matter any more what you did or didn't do because you couldn't do anything about it anyway. It was as if the rape flicked out my last hope. Nothing in life made sense any more; there was nothing to believe in. The world was out of control, so what really mattered?

"I couldn't cry. And since I didn't know how to deal with what had happened, I made a joke of it, trying to reduce its significance. 'Oh, it's just one of those things that happens.' This way everybody was comfortable with it and nobody had to feel badly for me.

"In a letter I wrote to my sister Judie about it, I concluded, 'With my luck I'll have a little Samoan running around behind me in nine months.'

"But underneath I was dying. I simply didn't know how to tell people what I was really feeling. And I think that today women are still uncomfortable talking about the experience.

"I didn't file any charges. We left for Japan the next day and I just wanted to leave the whole thing behind. I really doubt that I could have stood in a courtroom and recounted what had happened.

"And I've thought since that if I had been in court and anyone had said that I could have gotten away or that I'd asked for it, I would have either killed the person or gone haywire.

* * * * *

"I have never liked 'before' stories that sensationalize the past, that talk about the horrors in our lives. But I do use these stories in my testimonies because I feel that they prove the patience, the faithfulness, and the love of God, which is so much greater, so much purer than human love.

"Could you stand by someone, a husband, a child, or a friend through all this kind of rubbish? Could you watch that person hurt himself, hurt other people, refuse to acknowledge that you were there, and still love that person unequivocably?

"God did that in my life. And that's what makes this a love story instead of a horror story. The value of telling it is to show that God could take away all the tawdriness in my life and bring me out of it and then make my life clean and pure and good.

"And perhaps I'm the kind of person who had to bottom out, to fester in decay, before I could accept or comprehend God's message of love and forgiveness.

"When I speak to young people today, I tell them, 'Yes, Jesus Christ pulled me out of the pit; yes, He gave me new life; yes, He forgave me—and for all of those things, I'll be eternally grateful. But there is one thing He doesn't take away and those are the scars from that life. He takes away the pain but not the knowledge of it. The wound heals, but the scar remains. That will be with me for the rest of my life.'

"And I tell them to be careful, to avoid the things I experienced so they won't have pictures in their minds that won't go away, memories they can't erase. I know of physical relationships between people that I wish I hadn't seen. I have images in my mind that I wish weren't there. I have nightmares of being pinned down, and I get nauseated when I hear a woman scream on television. I am haunted by these things.

"I feel experienced and I don't want to. I know I'm clean and pure in God's eyes but I want to be fresh and clean in my own head. Yet I know that God is not punishing me. He's forgiven and forgotten, but He is using these things in my life to help me share them with other kids and keep them from having to go through it.

"So when kids say to me, 'I want to make a commitment, but first I'd like to try this or experience that,' I warn them, 'Sure, you can experience that, and sure, you can be forgiven, but you'll have to live with the scars and the memories for the rest of your life. And you will have more struggles and temptations because of them, because you exposed yourself to them and they were unhealthy.

"A Christian walk is difficult enough without adding more stones and debris to struggle through. Why not make it easier and more joyful by allowing it to be smooth and unencumbered, pure and spotless, inside and out?"

Part Three

PROMISES TO KEEP

The woods are lovely, dark and deep.
But I have promises to keep,
And miles to go before I sleep,
And miles to go before I sleep.

From "Stopping By Woods on a Snowy Evening"
by Robert Frost

Staff of nationally syndicated morning TV program, "U.S.a.m." Terry, host of the program, is seated in front with Scott Hatch, sports director. Standing, left to right, are Tom Mahoney, meteorologist; Bob Turnbull, health and nutrition expert; Terry Casey, news director; Steve Reid, features reporter; and Kathy Bullock, features reporter. (Photo by John Loizides.)

20.
A New Career

Freely you have received, freely give.

Matthew 10:8b, NIV

In the fall of 1977 Terry was in Atlantic City, co-hosting the Miss America Pageant with Phyllis George. Phyllis's manager, Ed Hookstratton, approached Terry one evening, asking what she planned to do with her life.

"I really don't know," she said. "I've been trained as a singer but I don't want the night club circuit any more."

Ed nodded in agreement. "Consider your future. How many successful fifty-year-old women are singing in nightclubs?" he asked. But he did suggest that she think about doing a talk show.

"Here is my card," he said. "If you're interested, call me."

Back in Milwaukee, the talk show idea got buried in an avalanche of Christian appearances, public relations contracts, and former-Miss-America jobs.

But the idea resurfaced a year and a half later when Milwaukee's WTMJ-TV approached her concerning a five-hour-a-week live talk show to be called 'A New Day.'

Terry accepted the offer. Eighteen months later, the show had shot up to the No. 1 spot in the ratings and Terry was named the "Outstanding Woman in Television, On-Air" by the Wisconsin chapter of American Women in Radio and Television.

"That honor really meant a lot to me because it came from my peers. I had plunged into an entirely new area, local television, and I really didn't know if I'd sink or swim. It was such a thrill for me to be accepted and even recognized by other women in the industry."

In spite of the status of being an easily recognized television personality, Terry refuses most requests for celebrity appearances, parades, ribbon cuttings, grand openings, style shows.

"I just have an aversion to those things. I guess I was so inundated with that as Miss America, I just can't do it any more."

Although she contributes some of her efforts to community involvement, the real bulk of her free time is spent in Christian endeavors, church responsibilities, Bible study, speaking engagements, crusade appearances, retreats, and prison work.

"I probably do four or five crusades a year with Bill Glass, former defensive end for the Cleveland Browns and now a full-time evangelist.

"Bill has a great interest in prison ministry, and through him I visited several women's prisons in California, one where Susan Atkins (who had been convicted along with Charles Manson and others) was confined.

"I gave my testimony and when I was half-way through,

Susan came in and sat down. She brought her autoharp and played several Christian songs for us that she had written. I had read her book on finding Christ in prison and I felt that her commitment was very genuine. It seemed even more convincing after I had met and talked with her.

"There is a lot of homosexuality within the prisons. It was a little disconcerting to have them coming in hand in hand, lying down together on blankets while you're standing there sharing about the Lord.

"One of the things I share with all the prisoners is that real freedom is something we experience inside of us, not something that has to do with being behind bars. And I tell them that I know as many people on the outside who are really locked up as people on the inside. I try to encourage them to try to be free in spite of their circumstances—free in Jesus Christ.

"Probably the most refreshing part of prison ministry is that these people have no façade. They have nothing to lose by being honest. They are already socially unacceptable. Consequently, there is an honesty and an openness that you rarely find in any other group. Conversely, they expect you to be honest and to level with them. As they say in prison lingo, 'You can't con a con!'

"I am so grateful for the gift of music because very often that is what bridges the gap between us. I usually do two or three songs—upbeat, contemporary things—before I share my testimony with them. That seems to get us on the same wave length, and they move along with me whether they think I have anything to say or not."

Terry appeared on the Greater Milwaukee Billy Graham Crusade in 1979 and interviewed Dr. Graham on her WTMJ television show. She has appeared numerous times on both "The 700 Club" and "The PTL Club." In the fall of 1981, she moved to Virginia Beach, Virginia, and is now a part of the Christian Broadcasting Network team, hosting a morning talk show, "U.S.—A.M."

While still in Milwaukee, Terry sang and spoke three or four times a month at Christian functions both in and out of the state.

"It's funny. When I first began speaking, I used to go to these things and say to myself in all sincerity: Lord, if anyone here has a need, I pray that you'll speak to them tonight with something that is said here. I still pray that this may be true. But I've seen and experienced enough since then that when I go someplace now, I also look at the faces of all those people and try to let myself really feel the weight of what many lives must be bearing. Because now I know that everybody out there has a need; everyone out there is feeling pain or concern about something. And it really doesn't matter if they're experiencing exactly what I am or not, because God's principles are the same for all of us.

"I feel a great deal more responsibility when I speak today. I look out and realize that I have a chance to be the vessel through whom God might speak. And I try to be really aware and let Him do that. I don't speak about my own life as totally victorious, but only that I'm learning and in the process of allowing God to work in my life. I try to remind my listeners that God moves us in and out of pain, and sometimes we must learn to be O.K. in the midst of pain. And with Christ, we can!

"It has always seemed more relevant to me to speak of the reality of the struggle and of God's goodness in the midst of it. People who are hurting need to know that victory can be had even before *our circumstances change.*

"When I first began speaking, I faced a dilemma which

I have finally resolved—the matter of accepting fees for speaking to Christian groups.

"When I was working for Wayne Coombs, I made quite a lot of money. After a year with the agency, I had made enough contacts that I was able to quit and just charge a standard fee. And yet it still bothered me, particularly when I kept running into the Book of Matthew where it says, 'You have received without paying, so give without being paid.'

"Finally, I reasoned that God had given me enough opportunities for community concerts, motivational speaking and former Miss America appearances that if a Christian organization wanted me, I didn't have to ask for a fee. And I'm happy with that. I don't ever have to refuse to go somewhere because they can't pay me. I simply limit myself to what I can do and make it a first-come, first-serve basis.

"One question that I'm asked a lot is: 'What do you want to do next? What are your aspirations?' And I'm always amused by that.

"I used to have a lot of human goals—ambitious goals. But I think that's changed in me now. This might sound like a cop-out, but it's reassuring to be able to take those decisions to God and say, 'Open the door or close it. You've got the key.'

"Before I would go anywhere today, I would have to know and feel that God had called me to do it, that it was where He wanted me to be.

"I don't mean that I don't have dreams. I do. I'm intrigued by network television, which is probably a normal aspiration if you're in the industry. A big part of me would like to do a film, a Christian film, with a message that I really believe in. I would love to record again. At one time, I dreamed

of a Children's Ranch: a place where kids could get away from the world, away from its values, a place where they could view the beauty of God's creation, get in touch with Him, and study His teachings. And I think a series of Christian books for kids would be fun.

"But He still holds the key."

21.

Commitment—A Process

> No, dear brothers, I am still not all I should
> be but I am bringing all my energies to bear
> on this one thing: Forgetting the past and
> looking forward to what lies ahead, I strain
> to reach the end of the race and receive the
> prize for which God is calling us up to heaven
> because of what Christ Jesus did for us.
>
> *Philippians 3:13–14,* TLB

There are many kinds of commitments to Jesus Christ.

They come in different sizes. Some last for two weeks, some for six months, some for a few years, and some for a lifetime.

They come in many styles. Some falter at the first sign of trouble; some are lost when the excitement of the moment wears off; some are replaced when something more attractive comes along; but some are strong enough to withstand any pain, any pressure.

"A commitment is not just a decision. It's also a process, a process we go through all of our lives. You don't commit your life to Jesus Christ and then just stand there and wait for something to happen.

"Sometimes I think we're too tuned into the decision,

and we forget about the process. We think, if we could just get that person to the altar, if we could just get him on his knees, if we could just get him to say that prayer, he'd have it all together.

"But the reason so many people pray the prayer of commitment and then go back to where they were before is that we don't take them far enough. We don't explain the ongoing process.

"When we make that prayer of commitment we are really saying to God, 'I want you to begin to make a change in me.' We are giving Him permission, yielding the authority to Him.

"And in Colossians we are guaranteed that position in Christ if we put our faith in Him, if we keep our roots deep in Him, if we build our lives on Him, and if we become stronger in our faith. But not if we are standing still.

"Having made my commitment ten years ago, it seems I should have it together by now, that I should be more consistent than I am. But I still find myself struggling, and sometimes I get impatient. I want to be farther along spiritually. I want to know that I've achieved what God wants me to. I want to feel I've arrived at the feet of Jesus. I want to be there.

"And then I think of Paul when he talked in Romans about the two parts of him. He said that the Spirit that is in the deepest part of his heart wants to do the will of God, but the flesh and members of his body want to do the exact opposite.

"So if Paul still struggled with this after his experience on the road to Damascus, I guess I shouldn't get down on myself just because I'm not Joan of Arc all the time.

"We need to know that there is a struggle, a struggle we'll live with all of our lives, but out of that struggle comes victory, victory in Jesus Christ."

* * * * *

"I think it was a little hard for my parents to accept my commitment at first, particularly my father, who was the Catholic member of the family.

"At that time, people really did feel threatened by what seemed to them new and perhaps strange expressions of commitment. It was a time of cults, Jesus freaks, and all kinds of groups doing their thing. And it was pretty much a California phenomenon.

"When I first came back to the Midwest, people didn't know what I was talking about. They were still sticking pretty strictly to traditional, formal Catholic or Lutheran or other forms of worship and expressions of faith. Later this changed, of course, and people all over the country began coming to Christ, expressing their emotions, and being able to be open and excited and articulate about their Christianity.

"I'll never forget calling my mother after I'd been baptized in a swimming pool in Reno. I didn't know my father was on the extension and I said, 'Mom, you'll never guess what happened to me. I was baptized!' And my dad said, 'How many times are you shooting for, Terry?' He was not too thrilled!

"There was plenty of tension and conflict when I first came home, bold and defiant in my new Christianity. I loved to argue with my father, and often embarrassed him if he misquoted Scripture, since I was pretty sure that he knew even less than I did.

"But gradually the Lord mellowed me and my parents began to see a change. I was a lot more honest and open and I was able to tell them how I felt and that I loved them.

"I gave my first testimony in Green Bay at an Assembly of God church. My picture was in the paper with a story saying that I was home from the Christy's and would be

talking about my new relationship with Jesus Christ. My parents came and brought some friends. When we left, I asked what they thought of it. My mother said, 'Well, it was different,' and my dad said, 'It's very hard for me to pray, Terry, when some guy next to me is talking out loud.'

"It also upset them when I said that I hadn't known Jesus Christ. They said, 'Terry, you talk about becoming a Christian, but you were raised a Christian.' And I suspect it was personally threatening to them to hear me say that.

"I continued to give my testimony with a feeling of boldness as well as inadequacy. I say boldness, because I had truly experienced Jesus Christ in my life. I knew what He'd done for me and nobody could deny me that. And I say also inadequacy, because people are used to hearing speakers who are scholarly about the Bible, and what did I know, what could I tell them after a nine-month relationship? But I gave them God's truth as I had experienced it and I tried not to worry about how much I didn't know.

"Soon after I became Miss America, my parents came forward and made a personal commitment when I was appearing at a Bill Glass Crusade in Fond du Lac, Wisconsin. I guess it's more evidence of God's goodness that today they are in a weekly Bible study, my dad reads Scripture and prays conversational prayer, and we're all together in the spirit and fullness of Jesus Christ."

* * * * *

"I have to give a lot of credit to Linda, my roommate, for helping me stay 'committed.' Linda joined the Christy's shortly before I became a Christian. As a minister's daughter, she had been raised in the Word.

"Linda had other Christian friends on the road and they were all so wholesome and so much fun that it was like being born all over again, clean and fresh. And for the first time in my life, it was acceptable to be those things.

"We'd all go to church together, and for an afternoon of fun, we'd get together and pray and talk, not so much about social issues, but about Christian issues: the goodness of God and what He was doing in our lives and those around us. I'd just never experienced anything like that before.

"And I was busy, too, reading the Word. Not an in-depth study but just reading and underlining and trying to take it all in.

"If Linda knew a church or pastor in the city we were in, we'd go to the church together and we'd be invited to sing. That's when I began singing 'He Touched Me,' the Christian version. It's the first song that Linda taught me.

"Eventually five members of our group became Christians. One night when we were in Las Vegas, playing the Sahara, we went to the lounge after the show to catch a black singer. He did a contemporary version of 'Put Your Hand in the Hand of the Man' during which he came down into the audience and began passing around the microphone to people to sing. John, one of our group, started clapping and singing, and by the end of the song, he had all those drinking, gambling people on their knees.

"The music kept playing and John offered a prayer while they were still kneeling, and all I could think of was what a wonderful world it would be if we could just hang on to that feeling. Then we sang 'He's Got the Whole World In His Hands' and 'A-Men' and it just went on and on and on. People were crying and it was a beautiful, unbelievable experience—right there in the middle of Las Vegas!"

22.
The Church Alive

> If you have any encouragement from being
> united with Christ, if any comfort from
> his love, if any fellowship with the
> Spirit, if any tenderness and compassion,
> then make my joy complete by being like-
> minded, having the same love, being one
> in spirit and purpose.
>
> *Philippians 2:1–2,* NIV

"I think that a lot of people today feel that their total responsibility to the church and perhaps even to God is regular attendance at church. But I really don't think that's a very solid overview or understanding of what the church is supposed to be to us or what we are to be to it. Rather I see the church as God's provision to keep us from being watered down, from being caught up in things of the world, from being like everyone else, to keep us a people set aside for himself. If we are to be a city on a hill for God, if we are to be the light in the darkness, the salt of the earth, then I see the church as the place where we find that strength and encouragement.

"Too many of our contemporary churches are dead—that is, the gospel is being read but the reality of that gospel is

not being lived. I think this shows up in our kids. I, too, heard the gospel all my life and it didn't mean anything to me.

"We must get beyond the technical information to the relevance of it. We must learn the concept of thinking through it, not just blindly accepting it, of understanding the reality of Christ dwelling in us, the enormous depths of our Christianity."

* * * * *

"We need to go to church to be edified and to worship God, to work on our personal growth. We need to seek an individually different walk with God and allow him to change us through the church body we are committed to.

"T. S. Eliot said, 'Commitment is a condition costing not less than everything.' So joining a church doesn't mean that we are just putting our names on a roster and saying we're members. It means saying, 'I am committing myself to you as brothers and sisters in the Lord. It means that I will encourage you and exhort you and I will expect you to encourage and exhort me. Worship is still very personal and reverent but we are also able to share openly with others what we are feeling and experiencing.

* * * * *

"Personal growth, to me, is what life is all about. Without it, what kind of trip would this be? I have to believe that we can have and be and do anything in our lives that we choose to do.

"In her book Come Away, My Beloved, *Frances Roberts writes of purity and holiness as coming from obedience,*

not from any whimsical wishing for them. They come from an act of seeking of the person of Jesus Christ.

"I think that one of the reasons we don't seek the person of Jesus Christ is that we have become such a complacent society today. This seems particularly true of the Christian society. We have such freedom, we don't have to fight for anything. Everything comes to us so easily.

"We don't seek Christ in our freedom and comfort. Yet Scripture says that Job, in the midst of all his turmoil, his physical and emotional pain, said, 'Though you slay me, yet will I praise your name.'

"I think that's the key to the whole thing in our Christian walk today—to be able to say very honestly to Him, 'God, I don't feel like doing this today. I feel crummy. I feel defeated. But you have called me to praise, and in obedience to You, I'm going to do that right now.'

"When I have done that, God has replaced the condition of my heart with one of praise. It's just amazing. When I have done that, it's pulled me out from under the waves and brought me back to where He is and I can see Him again for what He is. He can begin to work in me again because I've chosen to step outside of my self-pity and my tremendous need.

"In spite of the fact that Scripture says that God sees our good works as filthy rags, I think that many of us still work harder at our spiritual accomplishments than we do at praising God for who He is. We still struggle to comprehend that our only value is in who we are in Jesus Christ, not in our performance.

"In Come Away, My Beloved, *which is written as if God is speaking to us, He says, 'For like the sinner who misses the gift of saving grace through absorption in good works, so thou, My child, hast missed My sweet reality in thy frantic*

effort to please Me. As Martha in her desire to minister to Me forfeited My nearness, so thou hast done. My child, I have need of nothing. I desire only thy love.'

"I have always thought that we are called to sit at His feet, not to miss out on His presence as Martha did by her busy service. If we sit at His feet as Mary did, when He has something for us to do, we are there and can hear His voice and He can send us. Unless the busyness and service come from Him, they only keep us from knowing Him more deeply."

23.
A Precious Gift

Evangelism is simply one beggar showing another beggar where to find bread.

D. T. Niles

"Sometimes I look back at the girl I used to be and I realize that she's almost a stranger to me now. If I met her on the street today, what would I say to her? Would I like her? Would she like me?

"One day I did see her. It was in a women's prison in California. I was singing and she was sitting in the front row. It was like looking at myself in a mirror ten years ago. She had the same features, same hair, same eyes. I couldn't help thinking . . . there but by the grace of God . . .

"I had trouble concentrating on my testimony. My eyes kept drifting back to her, wondering who she was and why she was here.

"She looked so young, probably eighteen or nineteen. Was she a prostitute, a drug addict? Most of these girls were. But that sweetness in her face. How could she be?

"Afterwards, I pointed her out to one of the counselors. 'I just have to talk to her,' I said. 'She's the image of me when I was in high school.'

"The counselor brought her over after the program. 'I have to apologize to you,' I began. 'You're going to think this is strange, but you look exactly like I did in high school. That's why I kept staring at you this afternoon.'

"I liked her at once. I asked if she had a record player and she did. She seemed pleased when I offered to send her one of my albums.

"I mailed it right away, enclosing my address, in the hope that I might hear from her.

"The letter came two months later.

Dear Terry,

I wanted to write and thank you for the album. I shared it with the other girls and they all enjoyed it, too.

But most of all I wanted to tell you that a month ago I committed my life to Jesus Christ. I got out a few weeks after you came to the prison and I am now living with a Christian family.

So thanks, Terry, for coming and sharing with us. It gave me the courage to make my own decision to start a new life, a Christian life.

Yours in Christ,
Jan Smith

"Tears clouded my eyes as a surge of gratitude swept through me—gratitude for a God who exists in the deepest valley as well as the highest mountaintop, in the darkest prison as well as the most magnificent cathedral . . . gratitude for a God whose hand is always open, ready to lead us out of our darkness and into His light . . . gratitude for a God who has a precious gift for each of us, the gift of a new life."